Poems by First Ladies

THE FIRST-EVER ANTHOLOGY

EDITED BY MICHAEL CROLAND

Advance Praise for
Poems by First Ladies: The First-Ever Anthology

In this insightful anthology of poetry by 15 First Ladies, Michael Croland shines a light on the intimate thoughts and feelings of these remarkable and influential women. Well-written, well-researched, and chock-full of engaging personal background, *Poems by First Ladies* gives voice to what is in the hearts of these iconic women through their verse. A must read for history buffs and fans of First Ladies.

—Ronni Diamondstein, author of *Jackie and the Books She Loved*

Poems by First Ladies is based on rigorous primary source research and reads as compelling, revealing storytelling. This definitive new record contributes to presidential and American history while providing insight into the hearts and minds of these women we think we know. Every chapter brings a revealing perspective that defies their historical persona.

—Carl Sferrazza Anthony, First Ladies historian and author of *Camera Girl: The Coming of Age of Jackie Bouvier Kennedy*

What a literary cabinet of curiosities this book is! Poetry, history, literary criticism, even a musical score—editor Michael Croland has compiled a collection that is entertaining and inspiring, and often quite surprising. . . . First Ladies too often get overlooked and underestimated; this book lets their unique voices be heard.

—Jason Emerson, editor of *Lincoln's Lover: Mary Lincoln in Poetry*

Poems by First Ladies is a delight from first to last—and full of surprises. Meticulously researched and compiled by editor Croland.

—Feather Schwartz Foster, author of *The Colonial First Ladies*

Whether it's Louisa Adams, writing about her family, or Lucretia Garfield, capturing her White House view, the poems in this anthology reveal the personal side of America's political life. When Grace Coolidge wrote about her deceased son, she said he made her feel "the gentle touch." This book will do the same for history buffs and poetry lovers alike.

—Craig Fehrman, author of *Author in Chief*

This much-welcomed anthology gives a unique insight into the women, both well-known and underappreciated, who too served our country.

—Marilyn Singer, author of *Have You Heard About Lady Bird? Poems About Our First Ladies*

With these poems, each First Lady is revealed as the private woman she was walking the halls of the White House of her time. In this book, we can almost hear them whispering deliciously to each other, sharing their most personal thoughts about the world and their lives and husbands.

—Greg Lawrence, author of *Jackie as Editor*

Here is the beautiful raw material for a new presidential history, First Ladies' accounts of their lives in meter, rhyme, and verse.

—William Kuhn, author of *Reading Jackie*

For Louisa Catherine Adams, writing poetry was more than a means to while away the time. It gave her a space and form to explore the uneasy terrain a First Lady naturally found herself in. So it was with many others, who found humor and frustration and beauty in their unique situations. Through their poetry, this book offers an unusual and compelling reflection of American history.

—Louisa Thomas, author of *Louisa*

Poems by First Ladies

THE FIRST-EVER ANTHOLOGY

EDITED BY MICHAEL CROLAND

DOVER PUBLICATIONS
Garden City, New York

To Tamara and Robin

Poems by First Ladies: The First-Ever Anthology is a new work, first published by Dover Publications in 2026.

Library of Congress Cataloging-in-Publication Data

Names: Croland, Michael editor
Title: Poems by first ladies : the first-ever anthology / edited by Michael Croland.
Description: Garden City, New York : Dover Publications, 2026. | Includes bibliographical references. | Summary: "This first-ever anthology of poetry by First Ladies features captivating poems by fifteen of these remarkable women, including sonnets by Dolley Madison, valentines by Eleanor Roosevelt and Michelle Obama, and selections by Louisa Adams, Mary Todd Lincoln, and Edith Kermit Roosevelt"—Provided by publisher.
Identifiers: LCCN 2025020939 | ISBN 9780486853673 trade paperback
Subjects: LCSH: American poetry | Presidents' spouses—United States | LCGFT: Poetry
Classification: LCC PS591.P675 P64 2026 | DDC 811.008—dc23/eng/20250909
LC record available at https://lccn.loc.gov/2025020939

Publisher: Betina Cochran
Editorial Director: Peter Lenz
Managing Editorial Supervisor: Susan Rattiner
Senior Production Editor: Michael Croland
Cover Designer: Mark Voss
Creative Manager and Interior Designer: Marie Zaczkiewicz
Production: Pam Weston, Tammi McKenna, Ayse Yilmaz

Printed in Canada
85367501 2025
www.doverpublications.com

Contents

Acknowledgments

Thank you to Peter Lenz and Susan Rattiner for your support of this anthology. Thank you to the rest of the Dover team, especially Betina Cochran, Peter Donahue, Gregory Koutrouby, Andrew Sliwoski, Mark Voss, and Marie Zaczkiewicz.

Thank you to Susan Rattiner for your help deciphering handwritten poems. This was quite the undertaking!

Thank you, John Grafton, for your guidance.

Thank you to the Massachusetts Historical Society—particularly Hannah Elder, Gwen Fries, Sarah Hume, and Sara Martin—for guidance about writings by Abigail Adams and Louisa Adams. Thank you for providing "The rival chiefs—who all their life" and "Recipe for the Spleen, From an Old Woman," both by Louisa Adams, from the Adams Family Papers.

Most other poems by Louisa Adams came from microfilm of the Adams Family Papers. Thank you to Matthew Hartman, Jessica Infanzon, and Timothy Kohn from Stony Brook University's Frank Melville Jr. Memorial Library for your assistance with the microfilm.

Thank you to Earl Gregg Swem Library at William & Mary Libraries, particularly Carolyn Wilson and Kaitlyn Weathers, for providing Julia Tyler's "A Birthday Song" and "I would that I could add, love" from the Tyler Family Papers.

All selections by Lucretia Garfield came from the Library of Congress. Thank you to Mutahara Mobashar from the Manuscript Division.

Thank you to Benjamin Harrison Presidential Site, particularly Jennifer Caps and Angela Tuell, for providing "For a Friend" by Caroline Harrison.

Thank you to Harvard University's Houghton Library, particularly Naif Alrogi and Micah Hoggatt, for providing Edith Roosevelt's "Memories," "Dedicated to the Youngest Member (Nameless at Present) of the H. Denton Smith Family (Supposed to Be Written),"

"A Lament," and "On Some Apple Blossoms Brought to Me from the Country."

Thank you to the Library of Congress, particularly Mutahara Mobashar, for providing Edith Wilson's "To S. R. from E. B." Thank you to the Edith Bolling Wilson Birthplace Museum, particularly Adam Manuel. Thank you to the Woodrow Wilson Presidential Library and Museum, particularly Peggy Dillard.

Thank you to the Ohio History Connection for providing "Gone but Not Forgotten" by Florence Harding.

Thank you to Jennifer Harville, Julie Bartlett Nelson from Calvin Coolidge Presidential Library & Museum, and Colleen Stamos from Calvin Coolidge Presidential Foundation. Grace Coolidge's "Watch-Fires," "Communion," "Within This Room," and "Easter Sunday—1930" appear by permission of the Estate of Grace Goodhue Coolidge.

Thank you to Herbert Hoover Presidential Library, particularly Craig Wright and Thomas F. Schwartz, for providing all selections by Lou Hoover as well as two poems by Grace Coolidge. Grace Coolidge's "Within This Room" and "Easter Sunday—1930" appear by permission of the Herbert Hoover Presidential Library and Museum. The text of "Within This Room" is according to "Oral History Interview with Admiral Joel T. Boone," provided by Herbert Hoover Presidential Library.

All poems by Eleanor Roosevelt appear by permission of the Estate of Eleanor Roosevelt. Thank you to Nancy Roosevelt Ireland and Anna Olswanger. Thank you to Franklin D. Roosevelt Presidential Library, particularly Kirsten Carter and Sarah Navins.

"18 Million Cracks" is from *Hillary Clinton Haiku* by Vera G. Shaw, copyright © 2015. Reprinted by permission of Twelve, an imprint of Hachette Book Group, Inc.

Thank you to Vanessa Valdivia from the Office of the First Lady and Jacob Chaires from the Joseph R. Biden Jr. Presidential Library.

The sheet music for "The Quest," written by Grace Coolidge and arranged by Maury Madison, is courtesy of Special Collections Library, Western Kentucky University. Thank you to Nancy Richey and Allison Salmon.

Thank you to the Dolph Briscoe Center for American History at the University of Texas at Austin, especially Rachel Ledeboer and Marisa Jefferson, for providing information about and materials from the Maury Madison Papers.

Woodrow Wilson's "To E. L. A. on Her Birthday" originally appeared in *The Papers of Woodrow Wilson*, published by Princeton University Press.

Thank you to the East Meadow Public Library, particularly Christina Crocker, Mary Ellen Fosso, and Matt Longo for research help.

Thank you to East Hampton Library, George W. Bush Presidential Library, Georgia Historical Society, John F. Kennedy Presidential Library and Museum, the Los Angeles Public Library's Art Department, National First Ladies Library & Museum, the New York Public Library's Scan & Deliver and General Research Division, New York University's Elmer Holmes Bobst Library, Office of George W. Bush, Poets House, and Richard Nixon Presidential Library and Museum.

Thank you to Rachelle Moyer Frances, C. W. Goodyear, Kristie Miller, Katie Rogers, Sirpa Salenius, Zach Schonfeld, and Rebecca Steiner.

Thank you, Tamara, for your love and patience. You're the first lady in my life.

Poetically speaking, here's a shout-out to Robin, Mom, Jack, Nancy, Benjamin, Alan, Marla, Dan, Lisa, Zachary, and Zoey.

Introduction

Oh, my Easter Lily, I wish you were here!
(*What* a pity 'tis, Presidents' wives aren't twins!)
—Lou Hoover

The Bleeding Heart and the Easter Lily
May not be twins by birth
But they're closely akin
In love and devotion
And all other ties of earth
—Grace Coolidge

Most poems by First Ladies were not intended for publication. But First Ladies' poetry shines a light on their inner workings. It provides insight into their biographies and, by extension, American history. First Ladies represent the nation's evolving gender dynamics, and some of their poems document what life, with its peaks and valleys, was like for women at the time. To understand how First Ladies felt, read their poetry. This first-ever anthology of First Ladies' writings gives these impressive women a much-needed voice.

Scope and Origins

The corpus of First Lady poets consists of sixteen First Ladies. The fifteen whose selections are featured are Dolley Madison, Louisa Adams, Julia Tyler, Mary Todd Lincoln, Lucretia Garfield, Rose Elizabeth Cleveland, Caroline Harrison, Edith Roosevelt, Helen Taft, Edith Wilson, Florence Harding, Grace Coolidge, Lou Hoover, Eleanor Roosevelt, and Michelle Obama. Jacqueline Kennedy Onassis also wrote poetry, which is discussed in Appendix A.

Poems by First Ladies grew out of my previous two anthologies, *Acrostic Poetry* and *Poems by Presidents*, which were published by Dover Publications in 2023. *Acrostic Poetry* includes acrostics by John

Quincy Adams and Louisa Adams, and I became acquainted with the Adams Family Papers. When I worked on *Poems by Presidents,* I considered devoting an appendix to First Ladies' poems. Initially, I did not think there were enough—other than Louisa's output—for an appendix! For presidents, there was a preexisting foundation to learn about their poems, and I built from there. For First Ladies, I had to start from scratch, which was both challenging and fulfilling.[1]

While investigating their husbands, I stumbled across poems by Julia Tyler and Grace Coolidge and filed them away. As I fanned out my research queries, I learned about three books that consider First Ladies vis-à-vis poetry: *Lincoln's Lover: Mary Lincoln in Poetry, Eleanor Roosevelt's Christmas Book,* and *The Best-Loved Poems of Jacqueline Kennedy Onassis.* I had a critical mass.

To find other First Ladies who had written poetry, I looked through general books and other resources about First Ladies. The most helpful books—which I drew on for biographical information in chapter introductions—were Carl Sferrazza Anthony's *First Ladies: The Saga of the Presidents' Wives and Their Power,* Lewis L. Gould's *American First Ladies: Their Lives and Their Legacy,* and Dorothy Schneider and Carl J. Schneider's *First Ladies: A Biographical Dictionary.* If a First Lady was a teacher, librarian, or avid reader or worked in print media, I dug deeper. I looked for verse in every book authored by a First Lady.[2] The possible exception is Eleanor Roosevelt.[3] I searched online, checked out myriad library books, and got carried away with interlibrary loan. I was in touch with libraries and historical societies from thirteen states and the District of Columbia. Interest in

[1] Maury Madison compiled poems by First Ladies nearly a century ago. By the time I learned this, I had already found verse from all six First Ladies that he included. See Appendix E.

[2] This includes books by four of the five living First Ladies that were published within the last year. The canon of books by First Ladies is growing!

[3] It is difficult to assess the scope of Eleanor's bibliography definitively. I went through more than forty books by and about her.

First Ladies extends past American borders, and I contacted experts as far-flung as Finland and read books from places as distant as Nepal.

I did not pursue a full-court press for every First Lady. Few documents have survived for some First Ladies, including Martha Washington, so any poems she might have written could not be unearthed. As terrific as it would have been to include such a luminary, I knew that it would not be fruitful to conduct exhaustive research about her.

For the purposes of this volume, all verse qualifies as poetry. The standard described by Rose Elizabeth Cleveland in Appendix D does not apply. Casting a wide net includes as many First Ladies as possible, without subjective judgments about what is and isn't poetry.

Common Threads

Poems by First Ladies cross party lines and ideological views, and they span many topics and styles. They take varied forms, including acrostic, elegy, genethliacum, hymn, limerick, ode, and sonnet. They employ a variety of rhyme schemes—or no rhyme. Besides being political, they can be humorous, mournful, romantic, or satirical. Some selections are well-known, and others have never been published previously. The poems in this anthology span two centuries, from Louisa Adams in 1816 to Michelle Obama in 2016. Nevertheless, there are common threads that connect some of the selections.

Of the sixteen First Ladies who wrote poetry, nine had corresponding presidents who did so as well. Approximately the same number of presidents, eighteen, wrote poetry.[4]

Many selections address presidents. Julia Tyler, Lucretia Garfield, Florence Harding, Eleanor Roosevelt, and Michelle Obama wrote

[4] This includes the fifteen presidents in *Poems by Presidents* plus three others I discovered while researching the present volume. A poem by William J. Clinton is discussed in Appendix F. Selections by Millard Fillmore and Grover Cleveland have been added to the bonus materials webpage for *Poems by Presidents* at www.doverpublications.com /0486851532.

about their spouses. Dolley Madison wrote verse to John Quincy Adams in response to his poem. Louisa Adams composed poems not just about her husband but also John Adams, Thomas Jefferson, James Madison, and Andrew Jackson. Jacqueline Kennedy Onassis's "Meanwhile in Massachusetts," which delves into John Fitzgerald Kennedy's presidential ambitions, won over his family during their courtship.

Faith is a recurring theme, especially with Louisa Adams and Grace Coolidge. Louisa states, "I want the talent to indite/Poetic strains divine."

Valentine's Day was the occasion that most inspired First Ladies to write verse. Rose Elizabeth Cleveland, Helen Taft, Eleanor Roosevelt, and Michelle Obama penned valentines.

Some First Ladies composed poetry during their ladyships, including Louisa Adams, Grace Coolidge, and Michelle Obama. The White House was both the place where poems were written and the subject of poems. Lucretia Garfield discussed the White House grounds, Lou Hoover spoke about the building's "storied structure," and Eleanor Roosevelt addressed life at the White House.

First Ladies who wrote poetry were typically bibliophiles, and they often incorporated literary references into their works. Caroline Harrison helped start a literary club, and Edith Roosevelt was the secretary of one. Lucretia Garfield declared, "I have to read . . . as I have to live." Louisa Adams, Mary Todd Lincoln, Lou Hoover, Eleanor Roosevelt, and Jacqueline Kennedy Onassis were also exceptionally well-read.

Selections by two First Ladies shatter heteronormative expectations. Many Americans think of the First Lady as the heterosexual wife of the male president. Rose Elizabeth Cleveland—Grover Cleveland's sister, who served as the First Lady while he was a bachelor—and Eleanor Roosevelt both wrote poems to their female partners. Eleanor's relationship with Lorena Hickok, which was apparently amorous and physical, is explained in her chapter introduction. Rose's and Eleanor's romantic verse deserves to be included along with selections that touch on other aspects of their lives.[5]

Historical Overview

There is no explicit mandate for what the ladyship entails. This unpaid job is not mentioned in the Constitution. Many early First Ladies did little more than act as social and ceremonial hostesses. Many advised their husbands behind the scenes and were helpmates. In the last century, many have taken advantage of their platform to promote uncontroversial issues.

The role of the First Lady has grown dramatically through the years, reflecting changing societal norms and expectations for women. Especially in the nation's early decades, many First Ladies did not delve into political matters publicly. This volume recounts some of the key transformations along the way.

Not all First Ladies had similar experiences. Over the course of sixteen years, Dolley Madison shaped what the role could be. Lucretia Garfield was the First Lady for only about six months, as James Abram Garfield had the second-shortest presidency. Edith Wilson apparently took on some of Woodrow Wilson's responsibilities after he suffered a stroke. Eleanor Roosevelt expanded the power and scope of the position tremendously. Jacqueline Kennedy Onassis ushered in a telegenic era of celebrity.

---

[5] The discoveries of Rose's and Eleanor's love letters had comparable time frames. Hickok donated eighteen boxes of correspondence to the Franklin D. Roosevelt Presidential Library under the condition that they not be opened until a decade after her passing in 1968; they were unsealed in 1978. The journalist who went through the letters and connected the dots suggested they be "locked up again." The Minnesota Historical Society received Rose's letters as part of a donation in 1969 and removed them from a public collection because they "strongly suggest that a lesbian relationship existed between the two women." A researcher unearthed Rose's letters in 1978. Acceptance of LGBT people has changed drastically since 1969, when the Stone Wall riots launched the gay rights movement, and 1978, when Harvey Milk became one of the first openly gay elected officials.

There has not always been significant interest in First Ladies. There is scant focus on some nineteenth-century First Ladies. The first memoir published by a First Lady during her lifetime—by Helen Taft in 1914—flopped. Beginning in the 1980s, more historians, journalists, and other writers shined a spotlight on the role. By the early 1990s, the fields of history, political science, and women's studies had converged to give First Ladies' impact proper attention. The National First Ladies Library opened in 1998. In 2024, the first textbook on the subject, *U.S. First Ladies: Making History and Leaving Legacies,* was published, with a foreword by the sitting First Lady, Jill Biden.

Terminology and Style

The term "First Lady" was introduced at Dolley Madison's funeral in 1849. It has only been used consistently since 1911, thanks to a play titled *The First Lady in the Land.* Previous alternatives included "Mrs. President" and "Lady Presidentress."

While many people would define First Ladies as presidents' wives, other relatives have stepped in. Some scholars consider them First Ladies, and others prefer terms like hostesses, "stand-in chatelaines," and "Young Substitutes for First Ladies." This anthology counts Rose Elizabeth Cleveland and Priscilla Cooper Tyler as First Ladies. According to the First Ladies National Historic Site, at least fifty-seven women have been First Ladies.

Presidents' names are written as they appear in *Merriam-Webster,* which is the first resource for names recommended by *The Chicago Manual of Style.* Many First Ladies' names are omitted from *Merriam-Webster,* so I relied on *Encyclopædia Britannica,* the second recommended resource.[6]

[6] *Merriam-Webster* includes entries for "Martha Washington chair," "Martha Washington geranium," and "Martha Washington table," but not Martha Washington.

Per *The Chicago Manual of Style* and *Merriam-Webster*, "First Lady" is always uppercase; "president" is lowercase, unless it directly precedes a name.

Consistent with other books about the subject, first names appear for subsequent mentions of First Ladies' names.

The word "ladyship" is used, as in other works about First Ladies, without royalist or misogynistic intent.

Editor's Note

Each chapter begins with the First Lady's name, followed by her birth and death years. Her relationship to the president, his name, the ordinal number of his presidency, and the years of her ladyship appear next. In some cases, the years of a ladyship and a presidency differ.

Titles of poems are included where applicable. Some selections are untitled.

Louisa Adams was the most prolific poet among First Ladies, and she presented the most logistical challenges. I pored over Adams Family Papers catalog records, scrolled through microfilm from a bygone era, requested materials from the Massachusetts Historical Society, and transcribed handwritten poems. I narrowed down the selections from more than one hundred poems that initially made the cut. Because Louisa penned the lion's share of the poems in this anthology, her chapter warranted a different structure in order to provide adequate context.

Only women have been presidential spouses. Consider the candidacies of Hillary Clinton, Nikki Haley, and Kamala Harris, as well as Pete Buttigieg, in the past decade. It is not hard to imagine that the US could soon have its first female or gay president, whose spouse would be the First Gentleman. If the term "First Ladies" were no longer comprehensive and Americans said "First Spouses" to encompass all presidential spouses, this book's title would be outdated. I would welcome that development.

Bonus Materials

The bonus material webpage for *Poems by First Ladies* offers additional content of interest to readers. Visit the webpage at www.doverpublications.com/0486853675.

The webpage features an untitled poem by Louisa Adams. Links are provided for six poems by Jacqueline Kennedy Onassis, and a video shows Michelle Obama's recitation of her poem from *Poems by First Ladies*. Links are provided for a found poem based on Hillary Clinton's emails, as discussed in Appendix B, as well as two poems by Jimmy Carter about Rosalynn Carter, as mentioned in Appendix F.

All of the content linked to on the webpage was accessible as of this writing. Dover Publications and the editor of this anthology are not responsible if any of the materials are no longer available online.

Michael Croland
June 2025

Dolley Madison

1768–1849

Wife of James Madison, Secretary of State for Thomas Jefferson (3rd president), 1801–09
Wife of James Madison (4th president), 1809–17

Dolley Madison was the longest-serving First Lady. The widowed Thomas Jefferson relied on Dolley—the wife of his secretary of state, James Madison—to be the hostess. Following Jefferson's two terms, Madison was the president for two more, totaling sixteen years.

The most beloved of nineteenth-century First Ladies, Dolley was revered for being a gracious hostess at social gatherings and decorating the President's House. Her style straddled the line between elegant and simple. Before the British burned down the President's House in 1814, Dolley saved crucial documents and an iconic portrait of George Washington. When the mansion was rebuilt, it was painted white, hence the name White House.

Following her ladyship, Dolley remained invaluable. She arranged for the son of widower Martin Van Buren to be married so that his wife, Angelica Van Buren, could be the hostess. Dolley provided guidance to John Tyler's daughter-in-law Priscilla Cooper Tyler—who was the hostess when his first wife, Letitia Tyler, was sick and after she died—as well as First Lady Sarah Polk. At Dolley's funeral, President Zachary Taylor praised her as "our First Lady for a half-century," coining the term.

Dolley assisted her husband with his correspondence, acting as his secretary for part of his presidency and in his retirement. Dolley wrote thousands of her own letters—and three poems.

She composed two sonnets. With its rhyming fourteen-line structure, the stately sonnet is the most popular Western poetic form. It originated in Italy in the thirteenth century and has endured in English since the 1530s. "Sonnet on Mr. Webster's Departure for England" discusses Daniel Webster—a friend who was a senator and later the secretary of state—prior to his trip to England in 1839. Considering that Dolley lived through the Revolutionary War and the War of 1812, calling Webster a "grandson" of England is notable diction. "Lafayette" lauds the Marquis de Lafayette, a French aristocrat who fought alongside the American colonists in the Revolutionary War.

Dolley penned the final selection upon reading John Quincy Adams's "The Wants of Man." She celebrates the wisdom and beauty of his poem, deservedly so. "The Wants of Man" is the best poem written by any president.

Sonnet on Mr. Webster's Departure for England

Whom all delight to honor in their hearts,
   Webster! the warder of his Country's fame!
   Whom neither gold nor flattery can tame;
Who scorns to stoop to selfish, servile arts,
   Or lose, for power, a patriot's spotless name
Bids us farewell—for Albion's shore departs.
Bear him, whose mind is emblem'd well in thee,
   Great ocean! safety to the wish'd for mast,
A nobler product of our country free,
   Ne'er crossed thy pathless waves. With him we part
Whose shield is honor; birthright, liberty!
Patriot and statesman, both in him we see;
   His name is dear to every freeman's heart
And proud may England of her grandson be.

Lafayette

Born, nurtured, wedded, prize, within the pale
   Of peers and princes, high in camp—at court—
   He hears, in joyous youth, a wild report,
Swelling the murmurs of the Western gale,
Of a young people struggling to be free!
   Straight quitting all, across the wave he flies,
   Aids with his sword, wealth, blood, the high emprize!
And shares the glories of its victory.
   Then comes for fifty years a high romance
Of toils, reverses, sufferings, in the cause
   Of man and justice, liberty and France,
Crowned, at the last, with hope and wide applause.
Champion of Freedom! Well thy race was run!
All time shall hail thee, *Europe's noblest son*!

Lines Addressed to President Adams, on Reading His Beautiful Poem on the Wants of Man

Your *wants,* dear Sir, will seem but small,
  When they're compared with mine;
My single want outweighs them all—
  I want a soul like thine.
For all the wants that you may find,
  And yet ten thousand more,
Can never satisfy a mind
  So filled with Wisdom's store.

Louisa Adams

1775–1852

Wife of John Quincy Adams (6th president), 1825–29

The London-born daughter of an American merchant, Louisa Adams was one of only two First Ladies born outside the US. She was a central figure in the Adams political dynasty: the daughter-in-law of President John Adams, the wife of President John Quincy Adams, and the mother of vice presidential candidate Charles Francis Adams. She was depressed during her time in the White House. She organized dinners for thirty or more guests, but she frequently did not attend them. When she did go, she occasionally played harp or piano. As a bored recluse during those years, Louisa was a prolific writer, working on poems, a novella, and an autobiography.

She was an engaging scribe. Her writing is "emotional, critical, witty, and, in the Adams tradition, always frank," observed Margaret A. Hogan and C. James Taylor in *A Traveled First Lady*. Writing helped Louisa "fortify [her] own mind in its convictions of the truth." She claimed that she was sometimes "seized" by *cacoëthes scribendi*: an uncontrollable urge to write. She penned hundreds of poems, three autobiographies, letters, diaries, plays, and fiction.

Louisa did not intend her writing for publication, with the possible exception of her last autobiography. She would be shocked to find her verse in a book, as she claimed that her poems "seldom meet any eyes but [her] own." She did not rely on research. She often scribbled down poems in notebooks, diaries, and letters. She did not edit them or consider how they might look to a general audience, which explains her use of "warblers" twice in "My Children Ye Are Departed." She did not expect these selections to be compiled, hence her repetition of some rhymes, such as "love" and "above."

Louisa was self-critical. Reflecting on "Ode to Mr. Adams" in her diary, she bemoaned, "Still do I attempt to express my thoughts in poor and unmelodious Rhyme." In one autobiography, she said she had "no pretensions to be a writer and no desire to appear anything more than a mere commonplace personage with a good memory" and adequate observation skills. In another autobiography, she said that she "kn[e]w nothing of style or composition" and that readers would struggle "to extract light from the chaos which lies before them." She likely would have given the same assessment for much of her writing.

Louisa was too hard on herself. Her poems impressively convey her ups and downs. They capture the times she lived in, the family she adored, her devout faith, and her vast vocabulary and intellect. More than just shining a light on the prominent players she was surrounded by, her poems are invaluable documents from an important historical figure in her own right.

I. Historical Significance

The first six poems comment on events of historical significance. Louisa marks the passing of her father-in-law, John Adams, and Thomas Jefferson on the same day. She lampoons a loony political rival, John Randolph, with an acrostic. She calls her husband's successor, Andrew Jackson, a tyrant; elegizes James Madison; and addresses assassination threats. The political tension in these three selections stems from her husband's fight for people to petition Congress, which drew harsh reactions from defenders of slavery. She was an immigrant, albeit not from Ireland, and an apparently authentic voice comes through in "The Irish Emigrant's Lament."

Louisa professed that she was ignorant about politics, in line with norms for women at the time. She grasped far more than she let on, with clear understanding and strong opinions in her writing.

The rival chiefs—who all their life
Were striving to be even
In death renew their mutual strife
By struggling to reach Heaven—
Two Presidents in one short day
Behold this people—weep
Their fun'rals—none object to pay
The last expence—comes cheap—

Recipe for the Spleen, From an Old Woman

Judgement I will not recommend
Of sense perhaps a grain, or two.
Have flights of fancy, *villipend*
Nor mind of *all* you say is true.

Read all the jest books thro' with care,
Abusive sarcasm prepare;
Nor wormwood scruple now to steep.
Dark hellebore and snake root deep,
Of malice take a heavy drachm
Let envy there in mortar jam,
Pints of the gall you may infuse
Half of the dose take if you choose—

———

While venom from the tongue you spit
Tipsy, you'll think you've spoken wit—

Lines Written on a Recent Scene in the H. R. of Congress Free on Discussion and the Right of Petition 789 Feb[y] 1834

Down! Down your Flag! no more the fallen stars!
Shall wave triumphant o'er the nation's fame;
The stripes alone; a banner red with scars
Becomes the emblem of a tyrant's reign—
No more the Starry Banner proud shall fly
And boldly raise its standard to the sky!

But Earthborn; low its grovelling stripes shall hang
And drooping blush beneath its greatness lost;
While midst the raging din of hostile clang
No stars it sheds upon the warring host.
Its lights no more their vivid lustre yield,
The rights of man lie buried in the field—

What? shall the patriots' hefty burning zeal
Blanch 'neath the soaring Banner of the Land?
Shall Freedom's Champions lowly bending kneel
And basely crouch before a venal band?
Wave! Wave your stripes! your starry lights display;
They cheered your patriot fathers on their way!

Your fathers bled! your fathers won the race;
And wooed fair freedom with their parting breath;
Thro' perils wandered in the galling chace
Amid starvation, suffering, and death!!!
The stars and stripes in future times to shine,
Freedom's proud banner bears a light divine

Mourn o'er thy country and her rifled laws
Thy spirit guard, and still protect her cause
With golden thoughts posthumous, wake the mind
The words of wisdom yet shall save mankind
While on the page the ling'ring eye shall rest
Thy echoed voice resounds from mansions bles't,
A happy medium 'tween thy race and God
To save thy nation from th' avenging rod—

Threat of Assassination
1839

Dark terrors round my spirit cling
  And shadowing sprites alarm
While nightly visions active spring
  With vivid fancy's charm
Imagination onward drives
  Till wayward thrilling fears
Vainly 'gainst reason's power strives
  To check the gushing tears

Grant, grant! O God a helping hand
  And save us when we call
Protect us 'gainst the murderer's hand
  Support us lest we fall
When David called on Thee to spare
  By enemies assailed
Thou gracious Lord didst hear his prayer
  When he his sins bewailed

In mercy Thou didst bow Thine ear
  To list to his complaint
And from Thy throne in Heaven's bright sphere
  Didst see Thy servant faint
Thou didst Thy helping hand afford
  To raise him from the dust
O hear our cry in pity, Lord
  For blood! for blood! they lust!

The Irish Emigrant's Lament

Oh Erin! fair isle of my fondest regret
  Thy dear shore I bedew'd with a tear
Bright land of my fathers I ne'er can forget
  Thee, tho' blessings await on me here.

'Twas on thy green sod that my infancy grew
  Where joys pure and unheeded have flown
Where the scenes of my youth still to memory true
  Blend the roses of life with its thorn.

Alas! in the storm of political strife
  Ere the blossom of life could expand
The withering blast of destruction was rife
  Desolation was spread o'er thy land.

From my nation tho' sever'd by ocean's broad maze
  To thy welfare my heart faithful beats
While the eye of the mind will oft wistfully gaze
  On the image that charms while it cheats.

And fancy shall deck thee in verdure and bloom
  With thy rocks and thy soft flowing streams
Until death shall consign my frail form to the tomb
  I will cherish her magical dreams.

II. Family

The next eight selections focus on Louisa's family. Two poems about her husband precede an ode to her father-in-law. Elegies address her departed children, her son, her nephew, and her granddaughter, followed by a poem for a living granddaughter.

Poetry helped bring John Quincy Adams and Louisa together. He had been courting her sister when Louisa challenged him to compose a poem for her. The result stirred up feelings in Louisa. Throughout their marriage, he read poetry to her. One of her earliest poems, from 1816, is "On the Portrait of My Husband."

Louisa held John Adams in high regard, and he was among her favorite correspondents. She felt that he was the most welcoming member of the family.

Louisa knew loss all too well. She suffered about nine miscarriages, gave birth to a stillborn baby, and lost one daughter shortly after her first birthday. Of Louisa's three children who survived until adulthood, only one outlived her. Louisa addressed her devastating bereavement through verse frequently, especially for her sons. The process might have been cathartic, but it was not curative enough. Discussing "John's Grave" in her diary, Louisa explained, "Maternal love and Poetry have nought within their scope to satisfy the mind, when excellence worn down by misfortune is the theme, and the outpourings of the warmest heart seem cold, when they attempt a panegyric."

Her elegy for her nephew T. B. Adams should be read in the historical context of the First Seminole War. This accounts for the use of her epithet for Native Americans.

On the Portrait of My Husband

The Painter's Art would vainly seize
  That harmony of nature
Where sense and sweetness join'd with ease
  Shine forth in ev'ry feature
That open front where wisdom sits
  That eye which speaks the soul
That brow which study gently knits
  That soft attemper'd whole
That vast variety of mind,
  Capacious, clear and strong
Where brilliancy of wit refin'd
  Enchants the list'ning throng
That sense of right by God imprest
  That virtuous holy love
Of excellence whate'er is best
  Imparted from above
These Painters, if thou canst impart
  Shall fame immortal raise
And e'en the greatest in thy art
  Shall carol forth thy praise

To My Husband

Rise in thy might, with all the grace of mind
   And prostrate at thy feet the scorners see
Condemn'd to praise thee to their fate resign'd
   Unwilling plaudits speak the Lord's decree
Nor fear the scourge of malice and despair
Thy God will shield thee from their deadly snare

While wisdom flowing from thy parted lips
   With eloquence divine thy tongue has fraught
And youth enchanted from the fountain sips
   As bees from Plato's accents honey sought
A bright renown shall wreathe thy noble name
And new born worlds thy living fame proclaim

Ode to Mr Adams

He spoke!! the list'ning throng in wonder gazed
With rapt'd delight to silence hushed
The spirit stirring theme enthralled! amazed;
The blood enkindled ardour rushed
Quick to the heart with palpitating glow;
While wisdom's treasures from rich sources flow

He scann'd the past; the busy scenes of yore
The hallowed times of liberty, and zeal;
When freedom reigning o'er our western shore
With wisdom ruled; and stamp'd our country's weal—
When men enlighten'd, hail'd their nation's cause
And nobly taught both *liberty* and laws—

Assembled multitudes her claims sustain
The glorious work with zeal begun;
Braced, every nerve, to freedom we attain
The work is wrought; fair liberty is won—
Ye great departed! to your country true;
'Twas memory's halo he around you threw!

Time-honoured sages!! 'mong the good, the brave;
The hallowed Muse must pause to weep!!
'Twas thus he reared the fabrick of the grave
Where lie the honour'd in their peaceful sleep
Yet ye survive!!! Examples great and rare!!!
A nation's glory!!! Sacred to revere—

My Children Ye Are Departed

I have sought thee, I have sought thee
  Where the limpid streamlet flows
I have sought thee, I have sought thee
  Where the wild flower modest blows
I have sought thee, I have sought thee
  Where men in mingled tumult dwell
I have sought thee, I have sought thee
  Amid proud oceans' buoyant swell

I have sought thee, I have sought thee
  On the mountain's beetling cliff
I have sought thee, I have sought thee
  In the lightsome floating skiff
I have sought thee, I have sought thee
  On the wild sea's barren strand
I have sought thee, I have sought thee
  'Mid the beauties of the land

I have sought thee, I have sought thee
  Where the woodland bird delights
I have sought thee, I have sought thee
  'Neath the shade of starry nights
I have sought thee, I have sought thee
  Where the winged warblers sing
I have sought thee, I have sought thee
  'Mid the vernal sweets of spring

I have sought thee, I have sought thee
'Mid drear winter's ruthless snows
I have sought thee, I have sought thee
Where the summer solstice glows
I have sought thee, I have sought thee
In bow'ry shades of forest green
I have sought thee, I have sought thee
By the lake's expanse serene

I have sought thee, I have sought thee
Where the winds of autumn sigh
I have sought thee, I have sought thee
Where yon fluttering warblers fly
I have sought thee, I have sought thee
On the fleecy clouds of day
I have sought thee, I have sought thee
Where angels bide I trace thy way

John's Grave

Softly tread! for herein lies
The young, the beautiful, the wise;
Sorrow untimely nipped the flower
He sunk beneath her blasting power
But left a loved and hallow'd name
Tears of the poor! His living fame!
Lay him where the violets creep
Where roses clust'ring wanton sleep,
To woo the zephyrs as they fly
And blushing sweetly, fade to die—
Where the pale seringas nod
And shed their fragrance o'er the sod;
Where heartsease rich in beauty glow
And fair white lilies trembling blow;
There let the morning glory shine
To court the heavenly light divine—
The willow waiving o'er his head
To weep the relics of the dead—
The Cypress evergreen bestow
A mother's tears unceasing flow—

To the Memory of Lieut[t]. T. B. Adams Who Died at Fort Dade

Deep in the dells, where Withlacoochee's stream
  In silence rolls beneath the Hammock's shade,
Where Izard fell, awaking from the dream
  Of savage yell, and foemen's deadly blade,
The martyr'd victim heard the battle cry
And foremost rushed to death or victory.

Amid those darkling scenes, our gallant train
  In deep despair, with famine in their rear
The battle strife infuriate could sustain
  With deeds of valor, no renown to share;
No trump of glory their exploits to tell
No laurel crowns to point that *there they fell!*

And thou, loved youth, who thro' thy thankless toils
  A mother's doating heart could fondly cheer:
Midst dangers harrowing, whence the heart recoils
  Hast sunk in sickness on the fatal bier:
Oh! who thy worth, with trumpet tongue shall spread
And sing the praises of the sainted dead!

Poor martyr'd victims to a specious cause!
  Ye felt the wrong ye were compelled to do.
Where God defied, and all His moral laws,
  To Christian doctrine faithless and untrue
With treach'rous words inveigled, to betray
The savage proud *disgusted* turns away—

From infancy to manhood's early prime,
  The budding promise of perfection smiled;
A son's devotion hailed the coming time:
  A mother's hope the future yet beguiled.
In life beloved! in death for ever dear
Thy parting legacy the anguished tear

To the Memory of Georgiana Frances Adams

Sweet budding rose expanding into bloom
Nipped by the blight of death's relentless sway;
Upward, thy fragrance springing from the tomb
Immortal soars to light's eternal day
Angelic rose! bright in perfection rise,
Exhale thy sweets in Heaven's ethereal skies—

There midst the hosts that sweep around the throne
Man's mighty ruler who can all subdue;
Who bade us bring young children as His own:
Pure in their innocence as Heaven's soft dew;
Accept her Lord! renew the flow'ret bright
To bloom for ever 'neath eternal light—

To My Granddaughter Mary Louisa Adams

If words of love could but explain
  Thy grandmother's affection:
Her heart would greet the fervent strain
  And hail its true expression—
With fairy gifts she'd thee endow
  To cheer the mists of age.
Wisdom, acquirement, truth bestow
  From learning's purest page.

Fair sunshine o'er thy days should glide
  Beneficently bright
And dreams of happiness preside
  O'er the dark realms of night.
The arts should all their graces yield
  To gild the lapse of time
With stores of science unrevealed
  Treasured in every clime—

Religion pure thy heart should sway
  Faith thy unerring guide;
Virtue the glory of thy day;
  Humility thy pride;
The blush of modesty be thine
  To shield thy heart from ill:
Obedience filial and divine
  Thy duties to fulfil—

Such would I wish thee dearest one
  Ere life from me depart.
Thro' virtue's paths thy way be won
  With purity of heart.
Thus when thy span of days is o'er
  Sink peacefully to rest:
Thy sainted spirit upward soar
  Midst angels ever blest—

III. Religion

The next five poems are religious. "My Wants" is reminiscent of John Quincy Adams's well-known "The Wants of Man." A trio of hymns praise God. "Adam & Eve" focuses on Eve's role in the Garden of Eden.

Louisa was religious throughout her life, but her dependence on her faith grew over time. Experiences where she was anxious or sad, such as her ladyship and her sons' deaths, made her more reflective about herself. In *Louisa,* Louisa Thomas said that "her prayers sounded genuine but rote" compared to "the originality of her own language." This approach was deliberate.

My Wants

I want a spirit pure and good
    With zeal to persevere
Religious truths well understood
    Its Gospel to revere
While to my God in prayer I bow
    His gracious help to seek
That He His mercy will bestow
    His praise my tongue to speak

I want the talent to indite
    Poetic strains divine
To sing to words of living light
    The works that round me shine
The attributes of Earth and sky
    The wondrous ocean's powers
The race that thro' fair ether fly
    And all Earth's beauteous flowers

I want the attic salt of wit
    Its playful brilliant light
With corruscation flash to flit
    Like meteors of the night:
I want the youthful energy
    That sublimates the soul
Of wisdom the firm strategy
    That teaches self controul

I want the dignity of pride
   That high exalts the mind
The right unwearied to abide
   Of honour pure refined—
All cultivation ere design'd
   That rising upward springs
Imagination's taste refined
   That floats on angels' wings

I want the courage to pursue
   The truths I seek to learn,
To cherish all of good and true,
   With mercy vice to spurn—
That calm that meekly dwells with age
   That peace the world denies
The patient spirit of the sage
   The experience of the wise

I want a heart for others' woes
   A purse for their relief:
The tear with pity that o'erflows
   To soothe the pangs of grief—
To taste the joys of sweet repose
   Bless'd by domestic love:
With faith, in death my eyes to close
   In mercy from above

Hymn for Good Friday Litany

Saviour when in dust to Thee
Low we bow the adoring knee
When repentant to the skies
Scarce we lift our streaming eyes—
O by all Thy pains & wo
Suffered once for man below
Bending from Thy throne on high
Hear our solemn litany

By Thy helpless infant years
By Thy life of want and tears
By Thy days of sore distress
In the savage wilderness
By the dread permitted hour
Of the insulting tempter's power
Turn, O turn a pitying eye
Hear our solemn litany

By the sacred griefs that wept
O'er the grave where Lazarus slept
By the boding tears that flow'd
Over Salem's lov'd abode
By the anguish sigh that told
Treachery lurk'd within Thy fold
From Thy seat above the sky
Hear our solemn litany

By Thine hour of dire despair
By Thine agony of pray'r
By the cross, the nail, the thorn,
Piercing spear and torturing scorn—
By the gloom that veil'd the skies
O'er the dreadful sacrifices—
Listen to our humble cry
Hear our solemn litany

By Thy deep expiring groan
By Thy sad sepulchral stone
By the vault whose dark abode
Held in vain the rising God—
O from Earth to Heaven restor'd
Mighty re-ascended Lord
In mercy listen to the cry
Hear our solemn litany

A Song of Praise & Thanksgiving

Oh Holy Father! gracious Lord,
In Heaven revered, on Earth adored;
With grateful heart my voice I raise,
In language weak to sing Thy praise,
    With thankfulness and joy.

How many blessings hast Thou shed,
In bounteous mercy o'er my head;
In dangers past, by land, by sea,
Thy saving hand supported me,
    Still Thou wert ever near.

Father of Heaven, Thy grace instill,
Oh aid me Lord to learn Thy will,
With ardour I Thy mercies crave,
For Thou alone hast power to save
    From dread temptations dire.

When death had hurl'd his cruel dart,
And sorrow's sting assailed my heart;
Thou Lord didst consolation yield,
Thy powerful arm was then the shield,
    That saved me from despair.

When reason totter'd on her seat,
Thou gav'st me strength the stroke to meet,
Thy Gospel taught me to sustain,
The mighty woe, the ling'ring pain
    Which mortals must endure.

Still shield me with Thy mighty arm,
Guard me from life's seductive charm,
So great the blessings I enjoy:
Inspire my heart how to employ
The means that Thou hast given.

That my Redeemer lives I feel,
His suff'rings did Thy mercies seal,
As an atonement from above
He came to prove Thy Heavenly love
And all mankind to save.

Song or Psalm

Awake! awake my harp, my lute awake
   And sing the glories of the great high estate
The sinner yea! the scorner shall he break
   But blessed are they upon the Lord who wait

The righteous like a tree to Heaven shall soar
   No branch shall wither, not a leaf decay;
The ungodly perish and are seen no more
   Like chaff the wind shall scatter them away.

As trees deep planted by the river's side
   The godly shall their fruit in season bring
Washed by the lavings of the liquid tide
   Renew their blossoms every vernal spring

While on the law of God their hearts intent
   In fervid meditation they delight
In sacred worship every thought is bent
   To adore the God of everlasting might

The righteous in prosperity shall bide
   Blessings unnumber'd rich and great abound
Amid the congregations in his pride
   The sinful scorner's seat shall ne'er be found.

Adam & Eve

One morning sitting at my work I cried
How lovely, innocent and sweet was Eve
A lurking devil to seduce the bride
Exerted Godlike powers to deceive

The sophist's wily blandishment was wrought
With specious reason's charms to lure her mind
While eloquence divine his tongue had fraught
With wisdom, wit and sense and art combin'd

The fruit forbidden tempting Eve to taste
He saw his victory and glorious smiled
Eve ran to Adam with the fruit in haste
He ate! and by a mortal was beguiled

IV. Other Interests

Like "Adam & Eve," "Octavia to Marc Antony" shines a spotlight on a well-known female character, from William Shakespeare's *Antony and Cleopatra*. Louisa surely related to Octavia's missing Antony from afar, given her husband's frequent travels. Louisa was learned in literature and the Bible, as evidenced by her frequent references to them.

The final two selections discuss flowers: a bouquet and a jessamine. Louisa also penned verse about a lily, a rose, and a tulip.

Octavia to Marc Antony

Octavia writes thee; thy heart stricken wife
Invites thee home to share her wedded love;
Thy wished return great object of her life
Her prayers if granted by the Gods above.

Can dalliance charm thee to thy utmost shame
Amid the dangers of illicit love?
A hero conquered! honour! blasted fame,
Nor Gods, nor friends, nor country can approve!

Forbid it Heaven! Leave thy Syren Queen,
'Tis Caesar calls thee! 'tis Octavia woos!
The Nectar Cup, the bright luxurious scene,
The Circe banish, or Octavia lose.

'Tis true her radiant eyes may fondly gaze
Upon the polished marble of thy brow:
Her tongue beguile thee with its flatt'ring praise,
Her bosom heave with many a dulcet vow.

Her wanton smile with witching spell allure
And every fascination lend its charm—
Yet! yet awake! this passion base abjure,
Thy faithful wife's disquietude disarm.

Octavia pleads! no tear her cheek bedews
Her silent sorrows no complaints impart;
For thee alone each throbbing pulse subdues
The bitter feelings of a wounded heart.

Can Cleopatra deck thy stately bowers
   With love more fond, solicitude more true?
Her wily arts have shorn thee of thy power;
   Thy laurels faded can she wreathe anew?

Then what avails the beauty of her face
   The witching charms that lure thee from thy home;
Her softest blandishments yield but disgrace,
   To lead thee from thy glory to the tomb!

O listen! listen to my fond appeal
   My pride thy honour, and my life thy fame,
Faith whispers hope, while love that hope will seal,
   That proud Octavia may thy truth proclaim.

To a Bouquet of Flowers

Go sweet bouquet! adorn my fair one's breast
  Emblem of life, of beauty doomed to fade
Expand your lovely petals while you rest
  Exhale your fragrance 'neath the soothing shade

Life evanescent! richest sweets combined
  Invite the ardours of the sun's bright glow
With blushing beauties modestly conjoined
  Ye drooping fade ere yet ye budding blow

Withered ye die! no more the garish sun
  Reanimates the beauties of the dead
Thy little span of life of beauty run
  Immortal incense still thy roses shed

'Tis thus the amaranthine wreath of love
  Shall lead the spirit to a haven bright
Unite the soul with spirits pure above
  To live for ever in the realms of light

The Jessamine

I've watched thy fragrant buds
   Of beauty rich and rare
Expanding to the sun
   Beneath its fost'ring care

Op'ning with golden pride
   Their glowing leaflets spread
Bright yellow tints combine
   To grace each lovely head

A little span! they soaring rise
   In beauty's gayest bloom;
Then drooping fade away
   To meet their early doom

Emblem of youth and love
   Sad disappointments sway
Withers the germ of life
   To blight it in decay—

Julia Tyler

1820–89

Wife of John Tyler (10th president), 1844–45

John Tyler married Julia Tyler with eight months left in his presidency. She made the most of the limited time with her social events, leading to the title "Lady Presidentress" in newspapers. She began the custom of having "Hail to the Chief" play when the president entered at official occasions. She introduced polkas and waltzes to presidential balls. Julia used her coquettishness to her advantage, lobbying many senators to support the annexation of Texas. Decades later, "Mrs. Ex-President Tyler"—as she called herself—got Congress to approve pensions for presidents' widows.

Julia was thirty years younger than Tyler and, in his words, "the most beautiful woman of the age." During their courtship, her father passed away. She explained that this made her more interested in Tyler, who "seemed to fill the place and to be more agreeable in every way than any younger man." The age difference helps explain how the couple had seven children after Tyler's presidency—and how the last of their grandchildren just died in 2025.

Both of Julia's selections are *genethliaca*, or birthday poems. Julia wrote the first for Tyler's sixty-second birthday in 1852, concluding, "*Wit* I prefer to *Youth*!" In *And Tyler Too*, Robert Seager II observed that this verse exemplifies how "she passed off the age question with good humor." At Tyler's request, she penned the second poem three years later. She called it "an *impromptu*" and explained that, after spending ten to fifteen minutes on it, she "had no idea of accomplishing anything."

A Birthday Song

There is no month of all the year
  So fraught with joy to me,
As that which gives in annual course
  Thy day of birth to thee!
Drear it may be to other hearts,
  But sunny 'tis to mine—
Whilst I perceive, with eyes of Faith,
  My Image stamp'd on thine!

Full well I know thy Country's praise,
  Less sweet to thee will seem,
If oft I point thee to the throne,
  On which thou reign'st supreme!
Within my bosom's inmost depths
  Is held thy sov'reign sway,
The secret of thy power is one
  Oft told in minstrel lay!

There may be those with courtier tongue
  Who homage pay to me—
But deep the tribute Love compels,
  With which I bend to thee!
Let ruthless age, then, mark thy brow—
  It need not touch thy heart—
And whate'er changes Time may bring,
  I'll love thee as thou art!

Oh, we must be by Folly taught—
   Not read in Reason's lore—
If we can fail at once to own,
   The mind, man's richest store—
Then listen, dearest, to my strain—
   And never doubt its truth—
Thy ripen'd charms are all to me,
   Wit I prefer to *Youth*!

I would that I could add, love,
To wreaths that deck thy brow
A leaf of brighter hue, love,
Than shines among them now.

But if my *fondness* serves, love,
To *gild* those wreaths of thine,
Then will thy path be marked, love,
By radiance divine!

On this thy natal day, love,
I will renew the vow
Always to keep undimmed, love,
The lustre on thy brow!

Mary Todd Lincoln

1818–82

Wife of Abraham Lincoln (16th president), 1861–65

Mary Todd Lincoln was among the least popular First Ladies. She is remembered for tragedies—the Civil War, the death of a son, and Abraham Lincoln's assassination—as well as her perceived materialism and insanity. She was a more complex figure than those negative associations suggest. Mary aspired to be First Lady more than any of the others. During Lincoln's first presidential campaign, she took on a bigger role than a candidate's wife had previously, attending rallies, speaking negatively about an opponent, and welcoming journalists. She visited wounded soldiers in hospitals, raised funds for them, and donated her own money. She was a staunch abolitionist and helped steer her husband in that direction.

Since she was a young girl, Mary enjoyed poetry, especially works by Robert Burns, Lord Byron, and William Shakespeare. Mary and her husband read, recited, and talked about poetry together.

Mary's one extant poem jeopardized Lincoln's life. In 1842, the *Sangamo Journal* in Springfield, Illinois, published four satirical pieces lampooning State Auditor James Shields. Lincoln composed at least one of them. Mary, possibly with her friend Julia Jayne, wrote the fourth in verse, portraying the marriage of Shields to an undesirable fictional character named Rebecca. Shields was outraged and insisted that the newspaper's editor reveal the author. Lincoln took responsibility, but he refused to disavow the inflammatory material. Shields challenged Lincoln to a duel, and both traveled to Missouri, where dueling was legal. Friends got them to call off the duel in the nick of time.

Decades later, Mary admitted that she had written the poem signed "Cathleen." She explained that she "committed [Shields's] *follies* to rhyme, and very silly verses they were, only, they were said to abound in sarcasm causing them to be very offensive." She did not expect the poem to be published.

Historians had long debated whether Mary penned a poem titled "Little Eddie," but her authorship was disproved in 2012. To read "Little Eddie" and verse about Mary, see *Lincoln's Lover: Mary Lincoln in Poetry* by Jason Emerson.

Ye jews-harps awake! The ——'s won—
Rebecca the widow has gained Erin's son;
The pride of the north from the Emerald isle
Has been woo'd and won by a woman's sweet smile.
The combat's relinquished, old loves all forgot:
To the widow he's bound, Oh! bright be his lot!
In the smiles of the conquest so lately achieved.
Joyful be his bride, "widow's modesty" relieved,
The footsteps of time tread lightly on flowers—
May the cares of this world ne'er darken their hours.
But the pleasures of life are fickle and coy
As the smiles of a maiden sent off to destroy.
Happy groom! in sadness far distant from thee
The Fair girls dream only of past times of glee
Enjoyed in thy presence; whilst the *soft blarnied store*
Will be fondly remembered as relics of yore,
And hands that in rapture you oft would have prest,
In prayer will be clasp'd that your lot may be blest.

Cathleen

Lucretia Garfield

1832–1918

Wife of James Abram Garfield (20th president), 1881

Lucretia Garfield did not get to accomplish much as First Lady. After a pause by the previous administration, she resumed the serving of alcohol at official events. She planned to restore the White House and invite poets, authors, and artists. Two months following James Abram Garfield's inauguration, Lucretia came down with malaria. Two months later, the president was shot. A half year into his presidency, he died.

Lucretia had a lifelong love for the written word and intellectual affairs. She featured literary references in her letters and diary, and she adored the poetry of Robert Burns, John Milton, and Alfred, Lord Tennyson. In her youth, she clung to books while bedridden from a respiratory illness. As a student, she wrote an essay titled "Women's Status" for her school's literary magazine. Prior to her marriage, she taught Latin, French, and algebra. When her husband served in Congress, she was part of the Washington Literary Society. As a widow, she presented at her book club and partially translated Victor Hugo's biography of William Shakespeare. Until her final year, she took notes about her daily reading.

During their courtship, Garfield and Lucretia wrote letters to each other. When he left Ohio to attend Williams College in Massachusetts in 1854, they expressed their romantic feelings in their letters. As part of this correspondence, Lucretia penned two original poems for him. "To the Stranger" addresses her distant suitor "among New England's grand old hills" and is signed by "Ohio's Daughter." In "To James," she suggests that she is "the pearl" that "his heart" was "seeking." She offers "One pure heart which from its depths/Of love would smile his spirit's image back/Unchanged!"

After an assassin shot Garfield in 1881, Lucretia stayed by his side and supervised his medical care, vowing to "nurse [him] back to life." Americans admired her devotion. During the hot summer days beside "his bed of pain," Lucretia would look out onto the White House grounds. She composed "To the Poplar Tree Outside the President's Window," which is much shorter but far more striking than her earlier verse.

To the "Stranger"

Stranger, among New England's grand old hills
Whose hights to seek the blue of heaven rise
And in their voice of silent grandeur speak
The boast and pride of all her noble sons,
Dost thou from all their matchless glory turn
To thy far western home? And is *her* form
Of *milder* beauty *true*, yet to thy heart
Most dear? Ah well, it may be thus; for on
Her breath is borne a Mother's prayer or thought
Of anxious loving sister—while within
Her bosom many hearts are beating high
For thee; and near her hearth-stone lingers one
—Dark eyed, who now in dreamy thought perchance
Is looking on thee, and with wistful gaze
Would woo from thee a loving smile, or look
Of fond remembrance.
                                Then, though at glorious dawn
To meet Aurora's deep'ning blush thine eye
Is *orient*-turned, and thy whole soul is lost—
In wonder and delight while gazing on
The "fairer skies," and "greener hills" and streams
Of nobler flow, whose peerless beauties grace
New England's morn—yet when the breath of eve
Comes softly stealing o'er the western hills.
And Vesper, resting on her couch of gold
And purple, steals from thee a homeward glance;
Or when the dark browed night thy spirit lulls
To rest, with hush unbroken save by sound
Of merry rippling waters, or the swell
And dying cadence of the winds at play
Within the leaflet's home, we know that *then*

Thy fond proud heart to us is turned, and loved
Ohio's hills and vales are bright to thee
With gems from Memory's glit'ring store; and fair
Her skies with shining stars of golden hope.
Nor do we fear thou canst forget thy home,
Or better love a fairer one. Ah no:
But soon with eager step wilt haste thee back
To give glad answer to the voice that "shouts"
To thee a joyous "Welcome home again."

Ohio's Daughter.

To James

'Twas eve; and lighted was the festive hall
And merrily the voice of innocence
And mirth rang out upon the star-gemmed night
From happy hearts that now were gathered there.
But 'twas no scene where Bacchus vine-crowned god
Of revels rules the hour, or pleasures soft
Voluptuous queen her golden scepter sways.
No; 'twas a scene of purer truer joy—
This meeting of young hearts to consecrate
A parting hour, ere to their waiting homes
They hie away from classic shades where led
By wisdom's gentle hand they oft had strayed
And tasted oft her proffered fruits.
                                        Call not
Earth all desolate and barren save
Of thorns—a wild and dreary waste. Call not
This life all darkness, gloom, and woe; for there
Are flowers that bloom in every path, and e'er
The thorn a rosy garland wears; and there
Are sunny spots in life where friendship sheds
Her fragrance sweet, and love ope's to the light
Her soft, and blushing petals. Such an hour
Was this. Come with soft step and with me seek
Your dimly lighted hall. There where a tall
White column rears its stately form behold
A youth. We saw him as he mingled with
The happy throng—joy beaming in his eye
And gladness from his heart outgushing as
He spake to all kind words and smiled upon
Them warmly. Quietly from out their midst
He now has stolen; here, where reigns the hush

Of shadowy eve, to spend the passing hour.
But has he turned away from friendship's smiles
To pass this sacred hour alone? Ah, no.
Upon his breast a maiden gently leans;
His arm around her fondly and her hand
Within his own. No smile is parting now
His lips hove're. No word he speaks; but o'er
His brow thoughts glad, now troubled come and go
Like shadows of the clouds that chase the bright
Glad sunshine o'er the smiling fields of May.
Though young his life had strange reverses known
And many a page of sorrow had to him
Familiar grown, upon which others, though
Far older never yet had looked. In youth
His life had been a wild and wayward course.
Impulse his master fierce, and *will* the guide
Directing all his steps. On, on he rushed
In mad and reckless haste the downward way;
His giant powers of intellect fast bound;
His lofty spirit smothered in his breast.
But slowly kindling were ambition's fires
Which soon with quenchless ardor glow within
His breast, and melt his spirit's shackles off;
And free it upward soars on eagle flight.
Not pausing e'en where common minds rest down
Content; but proudly rising ever. Now
The world's cold breath of scorn, which chilled his soul
When first its wing was plumed for flight, was turned
To praise, and proudly flashed his eye as o'er
Him came the thought how far beneath him all
Her cruel hate had sunken, and how rich
The well-earned gifts of friendship that were all
His own. But mid these priceless offerings sweet

Had found his heart the pearl it evermore
Was seeking! One pure heart which from its depths
Of love would smile his spirit's image back
Unchanged! For he was mortal yet; and, though
When in his matchless might he soared above
Nor asked for sweet companionship, nor thought
Of friend however dear; still earthward must
His wearied pinions sometimes stoop. And then
As thirst the flowers for morning dew, which pale
And wither if 'tis not bestowed so did
His spirit thirst for love's sweet fountains; or
As seeks the prisioned plant for light, so sought
His spirit for the light of love to cheer
And guide. A gem with diamond brilliance once
Had flashed upon his sight, and in his wild
Impetuous boyishness he clasped it to
His heart "Eureka" crying. So he looked
Howe'er upon its dazzling light, to see
It brighter grow, *his eye* grew dim and from
His sight its luster faded all; and sad
He turned away and said 'tis but a dream
Of fevered Fancy's brain. There is no love
Unchanging, bright, and pure that Earth may know.
But still his spirit's yearnings would not cease,
And Hope's bright pinion fluttered o'er him once
Again, as gleamed upon him from afar
A pale dim light. He watched it trembling lest
It die. Nor dared approach lest when within
His grasp 'twould lose its radiance like his gem.
Long, long he looked upon that flickering flame
And gazing saw it brighter steadier grow.
—'Tis she within whose bosom like a star
'Tis set this eve he holds in fond embrace.

And as he turns his eye upon her mute
And calm—not even trembling though so near
His heart he holds her chilling doubt yet asks
If this is more than friendship's light: for there's
No *love* so seeming cold and passionless
His ardent nature knows.—A vision bright
The Past with every smile and treasured look
Of love before him rises.—Nearer to his heart
His heart he draws her—Folds her to breast
And o'er her bending whispers love, and seals
It with a kiss upon those lips which from
Her heart now trembling like the aspen leaf
Back echo all his lips dare utter. Bright
Angels hovering near their lips unite
And locked in love's embrace, their golden wings
They spread, and rise to Heaven's pearly gates.

To the Poplar Tree Outside the President's Window

You shimmer and you shine,
And your gracious light divine
To one sweet promise brings;
That from his bed of pain,
Mine own shall rise, to reign
The peerless one of kings.

Rose Elizabeth Cleveland

1846–1918

Sister of Grover Cleveland (22nd president), 1885–86

Rose Elizabeth Cleveland was the First Lady for the initial fifteen months of her brother Grover Cleveland's presidency—until he got married. A teacher, writer, and editor, the intellectual Rose apparently got bored while hosting White House parties, so she conjugated Greek verbs in her mind while receiving guests. She was a staunch advocate for advancing women's place in society. Controversies during Rose's ladyship involved wearing dresses with low necklines and going to the theater with a female friend but no male escort.

Rose's first published work was a poem in the *Independent* in 1884, and a second poem by her appeared in that publication the next year. Her first two books were published while she was the First Lady: the essay collection *George Eliot's Poetry and Other Studies* (1885), which is discussed in Appendix D, and the novel *The Long Run* (1886). She later wrote the introductions to several nonfiction books and translated *The Soliloquies of St. Augustine* (1910).

Rose's love letters to her partner, Evangeline Whipple, were published in *Precious and Adored* in 2019. According to the book's editors, Lizzie Ehrenhalt and Tilly Laskey, the lone poem among the letters "bears the hallmarks of Cleveland's assurances of enduring love" and includes "a striking, extended metaphor, in which Cleveland's passion is an ocean wave rushing to meet Whipple." Ehrenhalt and Laskey noted that the metaphor "leaves the impression that her emotion is an unstoppable force of nature; barriers of space and time . . . cannot block its path." The poem was dated February 11, 1894, and was presumably meant to reach Whipple on Valentine's Day.

Rose's best-known poem, "The Dilemma of the Nineteenth Century," was published in *Lippincott's Monthly Magazine* in 1887.

The lengthy poem consists of forty-one stanzas with ten lines each. It considers a peculiar illness for the character of Judith Von Stump and, metaphorically, the "woman question": women's roles in society. "The Dilemma of the Nineteenth Century" proclaims that women should not be restricted by "the chains of custom" and should instead be free to choose their own paths. In contrast to the view of presidents and First Ladies as the ultimate authority figures, Rose boldly declares, "Teach your great soul to call no mortal master."

And so, forsooth, I am told that in vain
I love you, because I have loved before?
Shall yesterday's drip of summer rain
beat back the sea from its shore?

This, which has rolled through a hemisphere
gathering strength each league, each hour—
shall it recede, because last year,
the sandy wave wet not a stone?

Nay—though you fly, it shall follow swift.
Face it, Ah, face too proud for dismay!
Make me a sign: a finger left,
and the storm's high tide will obey.

Sign me down—it will rest at your feet.
Sign me back—it will sweep to sea.
But no pale ghost of the past, oh Sweet,
shall stand betwixt you and me!

The Dilemma of the Nineteenth Century

I.

Judith Von Stump fell sick, or fell to ailing,—
   That was as clear as day to any one,—
And it was settled Judith's health was failing,
   That something was the matter, something must be done;
And so a meeting of the wise physicians
   Of either sex was called upon to sit
In counsel upon Judith's sad condition
   And charged to find a speedy cure for it:
From far and near they came, and saw, and—sat!
Of conquering I speak not: you shall judge of that.

II.

'Twas marvellous indeed how many doctors,
   Of every school and age, of either sex,
Came at the call,—from fierce concocters
   Of potions blue the gastric juice to vex,
To those exponents of a dispensation
   Whose sugar-coatings, redolent with ease,
Soothing and pleasant in their application,
   Outside or in, can never fail to please.
Nor lacked there those astute manipulators
Who charge upon disease like gladiators.

III.

Well, after some profound investigation,
The following were found to be the leading facts
In Judith's case. Her education,
Life subsequent, her birth, and other acts,
Were found to be correct, and well conducted,
And after the approved, accepted plan.
Mamma Von Stump herself was well instructed,
Papa Von Stump was no unlettered man.
She kept the house, he kept the store: together
They went to the right church in pleasant weather.

IV.

Or when it happened that a rain was falling,
Or papa's stock, why, then it is not queer
They kept the Sabbath day at home, in calling
On God to rain salvation far and near.
The Sunday columns of *The New York Weakly*
Gospel of Truth they read, too, at this time,
Receiving all its wise instructions meekly;
And both declared 'twas excellent, 'twas prime.
Thus, by this wise hebdomadal arrangement,
There came to these elect no sad estrangement.

V.

In such an atmosphere was Judith nourished,
And, at the proper age, to school was led,
Where all that genteel ladies learn was flourished
In pleasant breezes round her youthful head;
And, that no native airs or foreign graces
Should Judith lack, which fashion can invent,
To dancing-school (quite moral), where the paces
And bows of polite life are taught, she went;
And, as a finish to her education,
To boarding-school was sent for graduation.

VI.

And here she learned to calculate eclipses,
  And tell the structure of the earth beneath,
And estimate the measure of ellipses,
  And the idea, from Paley, of a heath
With a watch on it; and from Bishop Butler
  A confirmation of the Nicene Creed;
And from a little work by Mr. Cutter
  All the pathology nice women need.
And from Lord Kames she learned the critic's art,
And how the passions agitate the heart.

VII.

And then the august day of graduation
  Drew up the curtain on the pretty scene
Where Judith reads with nice articulation
  Her *Vale*, tied with ribbons in between.
Mamma Von Stump weeps fondly at its pathos,
  Papa Von Stump looks all around with pride,
And Judith bends her pretty head, while gracious
  Dr. Trigelgus hands the sheepskin tied.
The bouquets rustle, every one's elated:
The curtain falls, Judith is educated!

VIII.

It next appeared, the relatives decided,
  The proper time for Judith to appear
In social life had come: so she presided
  At a grand fete given for her eighteenth year.
The iron gates of upper-tendom tingled
  At Judith's graceful knock, and open rolled;
For from her taper jewelled fingers jingled
  Distinct suggestions of her papa's gold.
Judith's first season was a royal heyday,
She was crowned queen, and every day was May-day.

IX.

A year passed on, and Judith still was reigning,
  Her empire just a little less, 'twas said;
Young rivals said her beauty fast was waning,
  And old ones called her auburn ringlets red.
'Tis true that Judith (naughty Judith!), flirting
  Implacably, had cracked a dozen hearts
And broke a couple; "didn't mean to hurt 'em,"
  She said, and always gathered up the parts
And gave them back; and, singular, but true,
They all turned out again as good as new.

X.

Another year found Judith's empire shaken:
  The sceptre was departing,—that was clear.
The Grundys said (and when were they mistaken?)
  That Miss Von Stump's unparalleled career
Was at an end, and Judith now or never
  Must change her base, or abdicate in full;
No longer beautiful, now to be clever
  Was her last rope, and she must sink or pull.
She could no longer rule by beauty's part:
What now she gained must be by wit or art.

XI.

Here testimony all agreed, Judith was clever,
  And found her tongue as potent as her face,
With different results; for the endeavor
  To scathe with wit diminished from her grace.
At least the Grundys said that it was certain
  People began to think her sharp and queer;
Society considered her a burden,
  Too smart by half,—that truth was very clear.
So much for facts. Judith is twenty-one,
And our review of her past life is done.

* * *

XII.

What time was taken in the rapid mention
   Of these *few facts*, the doctors all sat round
With faces grave, in eager, rapt attention,
   Some dubious, some shrewd, and all profound.
The crowd was calm, save that I saw a very
   Young man at one time feeling of his heart;
I noticed, too, just then, a missionary
   Look somewhat shocked and give a little start.
After a pause, what next my tale discloses
Is the announcement of a diagnosis.

XIII.

And thus it briefly ran: "We find this woman
   Existing without life, at twenty-one;
Possessing all those forces which a human
   Nature can boast. The patient should be one
In robust health. Upon investigation,
   We find the nervous centres and the brain
A little strained; local ossification
   Threatens the heart, and yet no trace of pain
Is to be found. In fact, we are not sure
Of cause, and therefore find, as yet, no cure."

XIV.

On this a doughty doctor rose, and, calling
For silence, said, "The cause, sir, was a fall.
The woman fell in love, sir, and, in falling,
Got hurt a little in the head,—that's all.
And as to all your stuff about the heart, sir,
Nonsense! Among all woman-kind you can't
Single out one who don't possess the art, sir,
To make her heart as hard as adamant
If it suits her. Now bother all this chatter!
The woman is in love,—that's what's the matter."

XV.

In a great heat and much exasperation,
A little burly doctor then cried out,
"You're wrong, sir,—wrong! The proper explanation
Is quite the contrary, I have no doubt:
The woman's not in love, and *that's* the trouble.
Give her a husband, sir, a house to keep,
Children to rear, and this romantic bubble
Will soon collapse. Why, you must be asleep!
A woman, sir, is an absurd anomaly
Found anywhere but in the house and family."

XVI.

At this a murmur of shrill indignation
Arose from where the crinoline was dense.
A female here cried with determination,
"Sir, we insist on *truth* and *common sense*
And *science*, sir. The musty old traditions
Left to us by the elders will not do.
In seeking to improve the sad condition
Of our sick sister, we must learn to view
Her case in the broad light of progress, which advances
Beyond the pale of these effete romances."

XVII.

Amidst the tumult, one, with face exuding
With fat complacence, smiling pleasantly,
Said, "My dear friends, I hope I'm not intruding.
Our fair friend's sickness, it is clear to me,
Is one caused by unwholesome agitation
Of thought: in truth, her history
Makes clear that fact: it is an aberration
From woman's law. The patient must be free
From all brain-labor. It is foul, inhuman,
And out of nature, sir, for lovely woman."

XVIII.

Then up there jumped, with jovial air and bustle,
A little man, rubbing his hands with glee,
Who said, "The cause of all disease is lack of muscle.
Turn out the patient; let her climb a tree;
Feed her with bran; teach her to roar with laughter
All day; pack her in air at night;
Burn up her books, spill all her ink, and after
Ten months I'll warrant her all right.
A woman's proper sphere is vegetation
In air and sunshine, with good cultivation."

XIX.

The next who gained a hearing was a woman
Of visage resolute and purpose fell,
Who now proclaimed, in accents superhuman,
"The true cause of this illness I can tell,
And will. Our patient is a wretched sufferer
From man's injustice: you will please to note
The cause, 'tis soon explained, and 'tis enough, sir,
To make a woman sick, sir, not to VOTE.
She never told her grief, yet how it cankers!
Give her the ballot, sir: for this she hankers."

XX.

Immense applause, tremendous acclamation,
   Followed the speaker. Quickly then arose
Another voice, which said, "This explanation
   Is good enough, and true, as far as it goes.
Our Radical Committee of Research, however,
   Are happy to assure you that they can
Announce the final cause. Our patient never
   Can hope for perfect health until she is a MAN;
Which metamorphosis our noble science
Hopes soon to reach, bidding to doubt defiance.

XXI.

"Since in all sciences exact investigations
   Have made it clear that a desired end
May be attained by close approximations,
   We feel quite confident our female friend
Will soon have reached the last round of the ladder
   Reaching from woman's up to man's estate.
In truth, if Miss Von Stump long since had had her
   Feet free to climb, we do not hesitate
To say, this piece of ailing femininity
Would have attained a robust masculinity."

XXII.

The speaker ceased, and furious applauses
   Closed in about her,—or, I should say, him.
'Twas evident at last that the first causes
   Were reached. I heard, indeed, a dim
And insignificant remonstrance blowing
   From certain parts: the missionary men
Looked somewhat pale, but that, no doubt, was owing
   To change of air,—a little strong for them.
One glance at the reporters made me dizzy
With admiration, they appeared so busy.

XXIII.

The case being made clear, just how to treat it
   Was next the subject of prolonged discourse.
Some clamored, "Teach her medicine: you cannot beat it
   For making an already bad thing worse."
Others cried loudly, "Put her on a rostrum;
   To talk is woman's chief necessity;
It makes her comfortable; and no other nostrum
   Is suited to her taste so perfectly."
And others cried, with vehemence still madder,
"Just let her vote, and soon she'll climb the ladder."

XXIV.

Just then, amid the murmur and outcrying,
   Nature gave out. I slept, and, sleeping, dreamed
I stood at one end of a ladder lying
   Level across a gulf which without bottom seemed.
With purpose fell and step unhesitating,
   This perilous bridge from round to round I stepped.
The shore I left from sight was fast abating,
   And yet the farther one as distant kept,
Or seemed to keep,—an optical delusion,
I thought, and with this wise conclusion

XXV.

I still kept stepping on, and fondly hoping
   The longed-for shore soon with my feet to press;
Yet ever farther seemed its blue hills sloping,
   While still the one behind grew less and less.
On, on I went, yet by no footstep nearing
   The shore beyond; and then the night drew on;
Backward I could not turn: trembling and fearing,
   I fell, and, falling, woke. My dream was gone!
Gone were the doctors,—gone the crowd. All over!
And of the patient naught could I discover.

* * *

XXVI.

Yet, I have heard it said, the woman-tinkers
  Still wrangle o'er her case most faithfully,
And still it baffles the profoundest thinkers.
  "Who shall decide when doctors disagree?"
Ah, Judith! wheresoe'er we turn we see you,
  Your pretty, puny face, your helpless hands
Lying in graceful ease, while still to free you
  From chains yourself has forged, fermenting bands
Of yeasty quacks prescribe without a fee
For this sick woman of the nineteenth century!

XXVII.

Yet yeast is good. Now let no critic wonder
  We bid it hearty welcome and God-speed:
The air is murky, and the rolling thunder
  Proclaims a storm of which we stand in need.
No revolution ever boiled and bubbled
  Up from the stagnant pool of human thought
But it wrought good. The waters must be troubled
  Before the impotent folk may be brought.
And when an honest doubt is agitating
Men's minds, not far an angel calm is waiting.

XXVIII.

My creed is short, and easy of digestion,
Provided you possess those organs sound
And eager to discuss the woman question,
A subject strong and tough, as I have found.
I do believe a woman is a creature
Sent forth of God to run the race of life
As free of choice as man in every feature
And phase of this most noble strife.
The man has brain and soul and body; woman
The same; and this makes up the Human.

XXIX.

I do believe that life, for each, is just precisely
What each one's living makes it for that one.
Circumstance is the mould that turns us nicely
To just that shape we are when life is done.
Yet this is only half the truth,—receiving
Which as the whole is that most damning lie
Which fatalists may try to live believing,
But ever fail when called upon to die.
Behind the circumstance the soul sits, *choosing*
That circumstance,—accepting or refusing.

XXX.

A fact's a fact. This fact is past disputing.
Given a certain means, the end makes no delay;
Like causes, like effects. There's no refuting
A truth experience teaches every day.
Is demonstration wanted? What for dinner
Tickled your dainty palate this P.M.?
If cabbage, then I say, herbivorous sinner,
You'll find yourself a cabbage-head *pro tem.*
Cabbage you'll talk, or, if you live by scribbling,
You'll think and write just what you have been nibbling.

XXXI.

Not to pursue this somewhat homely figure
  To the inevitable bitter end,
We beg you to apply yourselves with vigor
  To that whence all these observations tend.
We live by what we feed upon. Our diet
  Makes us ourselves. I hold it true,
And challenge any reader to deny it,
  Four comes from putting two with two.
An angle-worm is just a mud wire wriggling;
A rose-worm's just a rolled-up rose-leaf wiggling.

XXXII.

Ascend the scale, and, as you run, remember
  That compound causes give compound effects.
You'll find this simple truth needs no defender:
  'Twill fit at every step in all respects.
And when you reach that acme of creation
  Where lordly man steps out upon the stage,
You'll find its most conclusive application
  Unlimited by pedigree or age.
A man is just precisely what his food will make him:
Learn first his diet, then you can't mistake him.

XXXIII.

Of course you understand I mean by diet
  Just all that feeds the man in head and heart,
Omitting not the stomach; for, deny it
  Who will, the liver regulates no meagre part.
Make out your formula, choose your affinities,
  Say, equal parts of ball-room, club, and horse,
So much flirtation, some few printed asininities,
  Et cetera, et cetera, in course,
And, if you strictly follow out your plan,
You'll have that "thing of hair and neckties" called a man.

XXXIV.

Or, given the brain for food and cultivation
  The problem of coiffure, the fitting of a glove,
And to the heart a serum of flirtation
  Instead of the rich, royal wine of love,
And for the stomach, too, such choice confections
  As best become her station and her taste,
All warranted to bleach the worst complexions
  And to reduce an apoplectic waist,
And you'll have one from out a countless myriad
Of pulpy, pretty Women of the Period.

* * *

XXXV.

Ah, Judith! send the doctors off! Look round you
  At Nature's bounty open to your choice;
Rise from the chains of custom which have bound you
  To slavish deference to Fashion's voice
And stale convention,—chains that must be riven
  By the same hands that forged and placed them there,—
Those same soft hands that God to you has given
  For better use than always "doing hair,"
Or advertising by their jewelled glimmer
Your heart a bait for any golden swimmer.

XXXVI.

Teach your proud will to make those nobler choices
   Which bring to soul and heart enduring health;
Deafen your ears to these contending voices;
   Look in your heart, learn your own being's wealth,
Its resource vast, its undiscovered treasure
   Waiting for these same idle hands to mine.
Dare not to sound its depth or take its measure
   By any human gauge or finite line.
Learn that the grandest of all God's creations
May not be bounded by man's limitations.

XXXVII.

Teach your great soul to call no mortal master;
   Reckon no other's reach sufficient for your own;
God's highway leads from all chance of disaster,
   Albeit each soul that treads it walks ALONE.
Learn your best uses: catch that understanding
   That heaven distils to hearts which, seeking, lie
In Reason's dusk; and heed no voice demanding
   Tribute to Cæsar. Fear not to defy
The loud *vox populi*. Hark! through its thunder
God's deathless diapason rolling under!

XXXVIII.

Choose work,—the work at hand. Nay, do not linger
   Where others wrangle over what just suits
To such a cast of brow or turn of finger:
   God makes no blunders: over our disputes
He smiles Godlike forbearance, surely viewing
   His own work good, though we indeed perceive
That the Almighty grossly erred in doing
   Thus with his creatures, and so, "By your leave,"
We say, "we'll do far better,"—while the tolling
Of Death-bells through Time's stealthy march is rolling.

XXXIX.

Choose Love, the marvel,—Love, the old magician
Whose alchemy divine transmutes our dross
To finest gold,—Love, the unschooled physician
Who, healing, takes no note of gain or loss.
Ay, choose thou Love: albeit in the choosing
Thou choose a day's feast and a life-long dearth,
Thou gainest still a greater gain in losing,
For Love and Pain are beings of one birth.
Love the Divine, Love the self-abnegating,
Love the Eternal, all Time antedating.

XL.

Choose Faith, the salt of work, the soul of Love, whose laughter
Chimes through an arid Present, o'er a barren Past,
With full sweet echoes from the great Hereafter,
Assuring work contenting Love, at last.
Faith in thyself, thy greatness surely knowing:
Faith in thy work, undoubting of its worth;
Faith in thy Love, ever more trustful growing;
Faith in the Pain that came with thy Love's birth.
Choose for thy soul such rich, sufficient diet,
And thou shalt find abounding health and quiet,—

XLI.

Such quiet as the sea knows where abideth
All moving life, all treasures rich and rare,
Such quiet as the untrodden forest hideth
Albeit all the singing birds are there.
So steadfast bide, whilst 'midst man's dreary chiding
Eternity is surging o'er the beach of Time,
And underneath thy feet its sands are sliding
Into that Ocean vast with sound sublime.
Its surf shall salt thy patient work's endeavor,
While Love and Faith echo its grand FOREVER!

Caroline Harrison

1832–92

Wife of Benjamin Harrison (23rd president), 1889–92

Caroline Harrison promoted educational and professional opportunities for women. She got her husband, Benjamin Harrison, to appoint a stenographer as the first woman on the presidential staff. In 1890, Caroline helped promote the Daughters of the American Revolution (DAR), which advocated for women's rights, and was the group's inaugural president-general. Her initial speech to the DAR, celebrating women's roles in the nation's founding, was the first speech written and publicly orated by a First Lady. That same year, she assisted in fundraising for Johns Hopkins University's medical school, with the stipulation that the school must admit women. She helped decorate the White House's first Christmas tree.

The daughter of a university professor, Caroline loved English and American literature and the arts from an early age. She earned a degree in music, art, and literature from the Oxford Female Institute. She was a multifaceted artist: a pianist, needleworker, and painter of china and watercolors. Caroline taught music, sewing, and the Bible. She enjoyed a weekly literature class. She helped found the Impromptu Club, where members read and discussed literature.

Beginning in 1847, Caroline drew illustrations and copied poems into a book she called *Floral and Poetical Album*. The collection includes one original poem, "For a Friend." She was seemingly inspired by Charlotte Wardle's 1841 poem "Stanzas on Hearing a Friend Regret the Advance of Age." For example, the line "And when the bright morning of youth has passed o'er" appears to be Caroline's version of Wardle's "And youth's bright morning beams decay."

For a Friend

If the sun of content be permitted to shine
On the happy or good may its rays e'er be thine
May the blessings of virtue attend thee through life
Unchequer'd by envy, unfettered by strife

And when the bright morning of youth has passed o'er
And the shade of its evening are seen at thy door
May the calm of that evening convey to thy mind
The pleasures of memory, for joys left behind

Thus each good which I wish shall attend thee along
While passing serenely through life's giddy throng
Shall protect thee, while journeying to nature, last doom
And e'en then shall appear as a star o'er thy tomb

a friend

Edith Roosevelt

1861–1948

Wife of Theodore Roosevelt (26th president), 1901–09

During her ladyship, Edith Roosevelt oversaw the renovation of the White House, separating the living area from the offices and begetting the First Ladies' Portrait Gallery. She made changes to White House staffing, including getting rid of the housekeeper position and hiring a social secretary, the first government employee to report to a First Lady.

Growing up, Edith loved to bury herself in books and adored English literature, especially William Shakespeare and poetry. She was a close friend of her future husband, Theodore Roosevelt, and his sister, Corinne Roosevelt.

During their adolescence, Corinne was the president of a literary organization, P.O.R.E. Edith was the secretary, responsible for copying contributors' works into notebooks. The acronym alternately stood for Paradise of Ravenous Eaters and Party of Renowned Eligibles. For about three years, the twelve-girl club met on Saturdays. Members recited their poems and prose while enjoying doughnuts and lemonade.

In *Edith Kermit Roosevelt,* Sylvia Jukes Morris deemed Edith's poetry "more complex" than other P.O.R.E. verse, noting that it "dealt with adult themes of loss, despair, regret, resignation and renewal." The following selections come from Edith's P.O.R.E. notebooks. In "A Lament," the group's secretary exaggeratedly bemoans the overwhelming influx of manuscripts, which she calls "Papers."

Memories

I sit alone in the twilight
In the twilight gloomy and gray
And think with a sad regretting
Of the days that have passed away

They have gone forever and ever
They can never come back to me
And while I am gazing upon them
Two faces I seem to see

A head with floating ringlets
Of brightest burnish gold
And eyes of violet tender
That to me will ne'er grow cold

Then a face with a queenly forehead
And bands of raven hair
With eyes of richest hazel
Deceit could not linger there

These faces rise before me
In my little fires bright glow
And them my thoughts do follow
In saddened and quiet flow

My sweet twin golden-haired sister
I can see her as when she died
And in those violet eyes I
Can trace life's ebbing tide

Small cause had she for trouble
Her thoughts they were for us all
Yes e'en when she felt the fetters
Of cold death hold her in thrall

My other, my noble sister
Enough had she to bear
Enough to streak with silver
The folds of that glossy hair

But round my waist is stealing
An arm and a voice so bright
Says, "Why is my little Amy
Dreaming so sadly tonight?

"I hoped you would miss me, darling
So in spite of the wind and the rain
I came from the city to see you
With Tom on the 6 o'clock train"

Now where can my blues have vanished
As I sit pouring out the tea
In the glow of dancing the fire
For Tom and Harry and me

Dedicated to the Youngest Member (Nameless at Present) of the H. Denton Smith Family (Supposed to Be Written)

Welcome! welcome! little stranger
To this world of toil and sin.
Welcome! welcome! our heart's portals
Open wide to let you in.

Cunning little tiny fingers,
Grasping at the empty air,
Cunning little feet so tender,
Little bunch of soft light hair.

Soon those helpless, tiny fingers
By life's thorns will wounded be,
Holding close the cruel roses
Plucked from life's deceptive tree.

Hold them, baby; as the poet
Tells us all to do who may,
And in every flying moment
Little one, enjoy your play.

A Lament

As I was walking down the street,
An old time friend I chanced to meet.
She said, "Why do you look so sad?
You look as you were going mad."
    I answered, "Papers"

"Why 'papers'? tell me child," she cried.
(I drooped my head and deeply sighed.)
"When last I saw your face, my dear,
You seemed not paper much to fear."
    Low groaned I, "Papers"

"Have you been going out too much?
I don't approve it, dear, for such
Wild gaiety must have an end—
But what's the matter? tell me friend."
    Then sighed I, "Papers"

"Yes, 'Papers,' happy girl," I said,
"Have nigh brought fever to this head.
I for the postman anxious wait.
Hope to find letters on my plate—
    It all is 'Papers'

"For to the Pore I always go;
I'm secretary there, you know.
The girls to me their papers send
And all unto the sad week's end."
    I sad, moan, "Papers"

"Some girls send in a day too late
(A fine their unsuspected fate).
Some never never send at all;
Them does our President appall,
  Commands their 'Papers'

"Dear friend," there said I, "oh, goodbye"
(The while a teardrop in my eye).
Take my advice if you belong
E'er to a club there friend be strong.
  Send in your 'Papers'

"Be not like *some girls* always last,
Their time for them too quickly passed.
And if to church quite oft you go,
Give up your club, dear, if you know
  You *can't* write 'Papers'"

My friend and I we parted there,
She with a most astonished stare.
Since then I've never seen her more
I frightened her so by my roar
  Of "Papers, Papers!!!!"

On Some Apple Blossoms Brought to Me from the Country

Some blossoms sweet were brought me
From the country fresh and fair.
And they seemed to whisper gently
Of sunlight and scented air

Of the place they grew so fairly
Of the gnarled old apple tree
On whose boughs in the short-passed winter
Snowy ridges might one see.

Now those boughs are hidden in blossoms.
There, sweet pink flowers unfold
And covered with youth and beauty
Is the apple tree gnarled and old.

And soon in the ripening Autumn
The mellowed apples red,
On the grass bloss'med the asters
Will be by those branches shed.

So may we. Though now untainted
By trouble, sorrow and sin
Like the rose-tinged apple blossoms
That flutter, the sunlight in.

May we through life's first summer
Take pleasure in joys as they come
Yet have, like the round, sweet apples—
Some fruit at the harvest-home.

My Dream Castles

I have many noble castles
    In the air
Buttress, battlements and turrets
    Showing fair
Clear defined each age-dark story
'Gainst a rosy sunset glory
    Pure and rare.

To my castles none may enter
    But the few
Holding to my inmost feelings
    Love's own clue
They may wander there at will
Ever welcome finding still,
    Warm and true.

Only one, one tiny room
    Locked they find,
One thin curtain that they ne'er
    Gaze behind.
There my lost ambitions sleep,
To their tear-wept slumber deep
    Long consigned.

This my lonely sanctum is;
    There I go
When my heart all worn by grief
    Sinketh low
Where my baseless hopes do lie
There to find my peace, go I,
    Sad and slow.

But my fairy castles still
    Bravely stand
'Neath the summer skies sweet
    Fancy land
Silken pennants flutt'ring gay
From their towers and wanton play,
    Zephyr fanned

Helen Taft

1861–1943

Wife of William Howard Taft (27th president), 1909–13

During William Howard Taft's inauguration, Helen Taft became the first First Lady to ride with the president from the Capitol to the White House. She started the custom of having state dinners paired with concerts or theatrical shows. After the *Titanic* sank, she led a fundraising campaign for a memorial. Her legacy includes some of Washington tourists' aesthetic highlights: the planting of cherry blossom trees along Potomac Drive and helping to get the Smithsonian Institution's First Ladies Collection off the ground by contributing her inaugural gown.

Helen once aspired to write critically about art and music, but her greatest literary accomplishment is being the first First Lady to publish her memoir during her lifetime. Although the publisher expected "to make a great killing with Mrs. Taft's book," *Recollections of Full Years* (1914) sold only 2,300 copies in its first two years. The book was quickly forgotten, as demonstrated by a 1939 *New York Times* review of Edith Wilson's book calling it the first memoir by a former First Lady.

On Valentine's Day in 1884, during their courtship, Helen wrote a short rhyming poem for Taft. She teases the lawyer about working so hard.

Leave your dull cases,
Let them grow dusty.
Turn to the graces! Till laughter effaces, their pages musty!

Edith Wilson

1872–1961

Wife of Woodrow Wilson (28th president), 1915–21

The year after Woodrow Wilson's first wife, Ellen Wilson, died, he courted and married Edith Wilson, in 1915. She was the first First Lady to have authorized Secret Service protection and dedicated office space in the White House. During World War I, she supported the Red Cross by selling war bonds and sewing. After Wilson had a stroke, Edith took on unprecedented power. Some historians have hyperbolized that she was the first female president. Edith contended that she did not make any public affairs decisions and merely assessed what was worthy of the president's attention.

Edith did not read much literature growing up, and she only had two years of formal education. In 1939, she became the second former First Lady to publish a memoir during her lifetime. *My Memoir* was primarily appreciated because of its focus on her husband. In the book, Edith admitted that she had "never written a line for publication" previously.

Edith wrote a limerick poem intended for Sterling Ruffin, her doctor and a family friend. "To S. R. from E. B." is undated and might not have reached its supposed recipient. In *Edith and Woodrow*, Phyllis Lee Levin called the poem "flirtatious" and inferred that Edith "seems to have taken the initiative as a young woman" pursuing Ruffin.

According to *The Penguin Book of Limericks*, a limerick poem is a poem composed of multiple stanzas using the limerick's structure and rhyme scheme. This was the golden age of the limerick, and Wilson was one of the humorous form's champions. He recited limericks during campaign speeches and a Cabinet meeting, and he authored two limericks.

After Wilson proposed to Edith, she sent him a letter that began with a poem. The first line is "Your dear love fills me with a bliss untold." Edith said that she had learned the poem "years ago." Considering that the source has never been found, some writers speculate that she wrote it.

To S. R. from E. B.

There was a distinguished M.D.
Who hailed from the state of N.C.,
  Who worked like a Turk
  And no labor would shirk
Though 'twas oft first for "sweet charity."

He drives thro' the heat and the cold,
While his neat hand the lever must hold,
  Of his automobile,
  While his fingers must feel
The bite of the breezes so bold.

A lady, in pity and love,
Thinks oft of these sad lines above,
  And at last doth decide
  (Even though he deride)
It is her place to fling down the glove,

Or *gloves*—for, indeed, it is *two*
She commends to his masculine view,
  And begs that he take
  Them *both* up, and make
To coldness a formal adieu!

Florence Harding

1860–1924

Wife of Warren G. Harding (29th president), 1921–23

Proud suffragist Florence Harding encouraged women to get involved in politics, and her husband, Warren G. Harding, was the first president to win an election where women voted. As First Lady, she actively advised him, including by insisting that he cut a proposal to restrict presidents to a single six-year term from a State of the Union speech. She advocated for World War I veterans, visiting wounded veterans at Walter Reed General Hospital every week. She worked in behalf of women, raising money for a clinic for pregnant women, supporting the first female federal prison, and hosting a women's tennis tournament on the White House grounds.

While Florence was not known for her writing, she did work in print media. She was at the helm of business, advertising, and circulation for the *Marion Daily Star*, the Ohio newspaper owned by Harding. She hired dozens of newsboys to deliver the paper, arranged for delivery to remote locations, upgraded printing equipment, and suggested story ideas. In less than a decade, the *Star*'s readership nearly quintupled.

In 1923, two years into his presidency, Harding died from a heart attack. On the first anniversary of his passing, Florence composed a touching elegy, "Gone but Not Forgotten." The *Harding Star*, published by several Harding-related organizations, said, "It, better than anything that could be written today, expresses the faith and loyalty of the Ex-First Lady." She distributed copies of the poem to friends in engraved folders with black bows. A few months later, after visiting her husband's grave daily, Florence passed away.

Gone but Not Forgotten

In sad but loving remembrance,
of my dearly beloved husband,
Warren G. Harding,
who departed this life, one year ago today,
August 2nd 1923

In the graveyard softly sleeping,
Where the flowers gently wave,
Lies the one I loved so dearly,
And tried so hard to save,
Husband how hard I tried to keep you,
Prayers and tears were all in vain,
Happy Angels came and took you,
From this world of sorrow and pain,
I would love to see your smiling face,
And kiss your fevered brow,
I would love to clasp you in my arms,
And have my husband now,
In my heart your memory lingers,
Tenderly fond and true,
There is not a day dear husband,
That I do not think of you,

Your loving wife.
Florence K. Harding

Grace Coolidge

1879–1957

Wife of Calvin Coolidge (30th president), 1923–29

Grace Coolidge was the first First Lady to cultivate a public image, appearing in photographs that were printed in popular magazines. After teaching at the Clarke School for the Deaf in Massachusetts decades earlier, she frequently invited the school's students and other deaf groups to the White House. She crocheted a bedspread for Abraham Lincoln's bed, intending to start a tradition that First Ladies would contribute mementos to the White House.

Grace began writing poetry while attending the University of Vermont at Burlington. She cofounded the school's chapter of the Pi Beta Phi fraternity, before "sorority" was used. She recited original poetry at meetings, including a history of the fraternity in verse. She later served as the organization's regional president.

Less than two weeks before the inauguration of Herbert Clark Hoover in 1929, Grace brought a poem—attached to a Scottie dog doorstop—to Navy officers. In addition to referring to the dog and their ship, "Within This Room" says the nation's capital "is dressed in its beautiful best" and Pennsylvania Avenue "bristles with seats." Grace notes that, with the Hoovers "coming to town," the Coolidges "depart/ With a pain in the heart."

Grace was close with her successor, Lou Hoover. When Grace was the First Lady, she selected Lou to pen articles about her childhood for the Girl Scouts' magazine. The next chapter features three poems that Lou wrote to Grace. In response to the first, in 1930, Grace composed one of her own in a letter to Lou. Grace warmly proclaims that the two are "closely akin/In love and devotion/And all other ties of earth."

Shortly after her ladyship, Grace started writing about her Washington years for *American Magazine* and *Good Housekeeping*.

The latter published her best-known poem, "The Open Door," in 1929. She penned the poem five years after her son Calvin Jr. died from blood poisoning at age sixteen, looking to him to "guide" her to Heaven. "I fully realize that the lines are poetic in thought, but not in form," she conceded. She said that the poem "wrote itself," and she hoped it would "spread comfort."

"Communion" likewise reflects on Calvin Jr. while praising God. It mentions the "green-roofed house" where Calvin Coolidge grew up in Plymouth, Vermont; the "small white church" where memorial services for Calvin Jr. were held; and "God's plot," where her son was buried. According to biographer Cyndy Bittinger, "Communion" demonstrates the "deep faith" that "kept [Grace] grounded as her son slipped away" and her "interest in the rural, natural world."

"The Quest" and "Watch-Fires" also showcase Grace's faith. They were published in *Good Housekeeping* and the *New York Herald Tribune* in 1930 and 1931, respectively. A musical score for "The Quest" appears in Appendix E.

Within This Room

Hark, hark, the dogs do bark,
  The Hoovers are coming to town.
The Coolidges depart
  With a pain in the heart
And Congress looks on with a frown.

The City is dressed in its beautiful best,
  The Avenue bristles with seats
The "Mayflower" rocks
  At the Navy Yard docks
While we laugh and partake of the eats.

"Only," a dog.

Easter Sunday—1930

The Bleeding Heart and the Easter Lily
May not be twins by birth
But they're closely akin
In love and devotion
And all other ties of earth

———

Oh, the D.A.R.s,
Well do I know the sound
Of their footsteps!
E'en the gleam of their galoshes
Has not escaped me,
And I declare unto you
That one wrenched back,
Whether acquired on foot
Or on horse-back,
Is more to be desired
Than three-thousand
Handshakes.

The Open Door

You, my son,
Have shown me God.
Your kiss upon my cheek
Has made me feel the gentle touch
Of Him who leads us on.
The memory of your smile, when young,
Reveals His face,
As mellowing years come on apace.
And when you went before,
You left the Gates of Heaven ajar
That I might glimpse,
Approaching from afar,
The glories of His Grace.
Hold, Son, my hand,
Guide me along the path,
That, coming,
I may stumble not,
Nor roam,
Nor fail to show the way
Which leads us—Home.

Communion

A quiet place, amid enfolding hills,
Green grass beneath my feet
And overhead, blue sky
With in between long, distances
To dream about;

Within a green-roofed house,
Sweet memories blessing every room;
Across the road, a small white church
Whose open door invites to prayer;

And just around the turn,
On yonder hill, God's plot
Where sleep His dead—and mine—
Beneath two guardian pines;

So dear a place on earth,
So near the home called heaven;

And yet, the unwise ask,
Where is thy God.

The Quest

Crossing the uplands of time,
Skirting the borders of night,
Scaling the face of the peak of dreams,
We enter the region of light,
And hastening on, with eager intent,
Arrive at the rainbow's end,
And there uncover the pot of gold
Buried deep in the heart of a friend.

Watch-Fires

Love was not given the human heart
  For careless dealing.
Its spark was lit that man might know
  Divine revealing.

Heaped up with sacrificial brands,
  The flame, in mounting,
Enkindles other hearts with love,
  Beyond the counting.

Reflected back into each life,
  These vast fires, glowing,
Do then become the perfect love
  Of Christ's bestowing.

Lou Hoover

1874–1944

Wife of Herbert Clark Hoover (31st president), 1929–33

Lou Hoover was the first First Lady to get publicly involved in a presidential administration, offer frequent interviews, and appear on the radio. She founded Rapidan Camp, the original presidential retreat. During the Great Depression, she championed her husband's economic plan in her letters, encouraged women to help the needy, and pressured the National Congress of Parents and Teachers to provide clothing and books so that children could remain in school.

As a child, Lou was an avid reader and was active in a literary club. She began writing prolifically as a teenager. After becoming the first woman in the US to earn a geology degree—and meeting Herbert Clark Hoover in school—the couple collaborated on a translation from Latin of *Agricola de re Metallica,* a sixteenth-century mining manual. She focused on the language, and he concentrated on the scientific aspects. She is the only First Lady to receive an honorary degree prior to her ladyship.

Lou loved the outdoors, as reflected in her 1895 poem, "Dedicated to Dorothy Ethel Bishop." In *A Woman of Adventure,* Annette B. Dunlap noted that Lou's writings from this period "reveal a keen observer of human nature and Mother Nature."

Lou wrote "Going, and Coming" when her organized secretary, Philippi Harding Butler, resigned and got married in 1924. Butler became Lou's White House secretary in 1931.

In 1930, when the White House was renovated, Lou kept the wood that was discarded. For Christmas, she gifted it—in the form of wooden boxes, bookends, and letter openers—to friends and staff. She enclosed her poem "Recollections of a Piece of Wood," sharing the perspective of wood after "a century buried deep within the White House walls."

Lou had a strong bond with her predecessor, Grace Coolidge, who guided Lou on First Lady duties. They gave each other flower nicknames, with Lou calling Grace "Lily" and Grace referring to Lou as "Bleeding Heart." Lou wrote three poems to Grace. In a poem for Easter in 1930, Lou declares, "*What* a pity 'tis, Presidents' wives aren't twins!" After Grace's husband, Calvin Coolidge, died in 1933, Lou composed two poems inviting Grace to visit—once shortly before the end of Hoover's presidency and once right afterward.

Lou was involved with the Girl Scouts for three decades, including stints as president of the organization before and after she was the First Lady. She believed that the group "teaches play, individual helpfulness, and citizenship." She wrote "A Greeting to the Girl Scouts and Leaders of Brooklyn" when she was on a train in Utah in 1936, while she was the president.

Dedicated to Dorothy Ethel Bishop

Oh the wind it howled like some wicked gnome
 As we made our hurried flight,
But we took out our blankets and never came home
 Thro' all the live-long night.

But we slept, slept, slept
In that little cañon
Way on the other side of Black Mountain.

But time must pass,
And there came, alas,
Those dreaded fears with the gloaming.

But draw round the campfire, and don't be afraid,
Of the horses' neigh, or the hoot owls' raid,
For what care we tho' the wild cat be a-roaming.

For in the light of the bright flames dancing,
Oh, how joyous all appears;
Sweet guitar, and warrior's prancing,
Put to flight all fears.

 Ah, ha, ha, ha, ha!
What tho' fiercely the wind rages,
We will ne'er declare 'tis cold,
Could we not sleep thus for ages,
Snugly in our blankets rolled!
Come then on dreams pinions soar
While the moon and stars watch o'er.
For too soon the dawn awakes us
And, 'tis sad, but true, that then
Thoughts of breakfast will o'ertake us
And we'll long for "dope" again
Up, then, help prepare the feast.

Then pile up the wood as high as 'twill stand,
And put the coffee on.
With dope and quail and toast at hand
Keen hunger'll soon be gone,
Then we'll eat, eat, eat, till our plate's empty,
Without one thought of University.

But time will pass,
And there comes, alas,
That sad, sad hour to pack, oh!

But load up the wagon and clamber in,
And we'll try to forget midst the merry din
That many a weary day must pass
  Ere we're back, oh!

Going, and Coming

Gone are the days when my papers all were straight,—
Gone are the times when appointments ne'er were late,—
Gone are the carbons beneath the paper weight,—
  I hear their wailing voices calling, "Oh P.H."

    She's going, she's going,
      Where the bounding billows play.
    I hear their roaring voices calling,
      "P.H.! Hey!"

Come has a lad who has merry eyes and blue,—
Come with a uniform to match Phil's Scout one, too,—
Come with a dash that has taken her away,—
  She heard his pleading voice a-calling, "Come, P.H."

    "Come, Phillie! Come, Philippi!
      Let's sail us far away.
    Let's go to Chiner on a liner!
      Come, P.H."

Recollections of a Piece of Wood

A pine tree on the hills of Maryland,—through many summers' heats and winters' snows.
Felled, carted, quartered, sawn, a metamorphosis within a week.
And then a century buried deep within the White House walls.— unseen, unsung, but one of myriads holding firm together the storied structure.
Until, a new age came and replaced steel for wood.
Then months upon the dump-heap,—the dump cart actually arrived for one last ride,—
And then a rescue. Now here I rest upon your desk for a short space; until,—the wastebasket and the fire.
Then once again I'll go,—free smoke before free wind,—to touch again the hills of Maryland.

Oh my fairest Lily,
  I miss you so.
Oh my fairest Lily,
  when the south winds blow,
When the towering needle
  points the blue,
When robins and starlings
  are calling for you,
When thro' the magnolia
  the red birds dart,
Oh my fairest Lily!
    Your B.H.

An Easter Lily breaks bud by my couch.
  (The oaks are gathering below.)
The first white flower looks wonderingly forth.
  (The strains of the Mariner come up soft and low.)

The Easter Lily looks out at the rain
  (Umbrellas and galoshes in the East corridor).
Oh, my Easter Lily, I wish you were here!
  (*What* a pity 'tis, Presidents' wives aren't twins!)

(Truth was happier than rhymes in the last lines!)

Up and down and around about
The house, you have gone with me.
In years gone by it has often been,
But in these days, constantly.

The house of beauty, the house of joy,
The house of sadness, of history.
Some ghosts are stately, and some grotesque
Some tragic, some gay, some humoresque.

Dear,—halls, and stairs and chambers wide
Still treasure the touch of your footstep light
And long for another glimpse of you.

My fair Lily—

The Spring has come up from the ocean
And started East over the peaks.
The lilacs are wild on the mountain.
Nearly gone are the almond and peach.

The humming birds rise from the cherries,
To be lost in the blue overhead.
The wisteria drips from its trellis.
Pomegranate blooms show their red.

Now, soon, in Nevada and Kansas,
In Massachusetts and Northamp,
Winter will loosen its last fangs as
Summer 'gins trimming her lamp.
(I dont quite know why—but it sounds mystic, and rhymes!)

So, Lily, 'tis time you were moving,
Packing up for a picnic or two.
The whole world's before you for wand'ring,
But westward's the right thing to do.

We've a bed on the porch 'neath the stars, here.
And a tray on the roof 'neath the sun.
There's an old car with a patch on the cover,
And one with *no* cover,—more fun!

There's a glimpse of the bay from your bed, dear.
The college chimes drowse in your ear.
You golf or you swim, or you wind 'round the rim,
To see the sun sink in the sea.

Alas, it is 'most time for luncheon,
I can't Spring-feve any more today.
But know, dear, that everything's ready,—
We hope you'll soon be on your way.

We'll meet you at Oakland or San Francisco
With a car, and most welcoming arms.
And we hope you will stay a long time
And love all the Campus's charms.

Meantime,
Your own loving
'Heart.

A Greeting to the Girl Scouts and Leaders of Brooklyn

A file of mail upon the table before me,—awaiting answer.
On top the gay cover of Brooklyn's Bulletin,—and your friendly
note,
oh, Nellie Truman.

And so I turn my thoughts eastward again, and my mind
To framing into words the more than cordial greetings that are in my
heart
For the Girl Scouts of Brooklyn.

But alas,—a window of the speeding train is not two feet away!
The immediate, changing, scene of this Far West, in winter,
Pulls 'gainst the memories of Brooklyn,—still in winter, too,
Altho' my own garden, toward which we rush,
Is now crowded with daffodils and iris, tulips and jonquils, jasmine
and wisteria.

A mountain looms snow-white now
Against the violet blue of clearing skies.
And toward its greying base trails may be outlined
Leading to mining dumps.

Nearby the sugar-powdered bush
Rises above the clear white of flat ground.
A magpie, jaunty, lights on broken bough of sparse-leaved
cotton-wood.

Sudden, a little river runs under the rails, twists away, turns and
returns,
Low willows fringing its banks, whose catkins are great powder puffs
of snow.

A chipmunk scurries into the tufts of pale beige grass.
Is it a bluebird circling to that wire?
Sky almost the shade of the shadows on the snow.
White and grey and beige, and snow-blue above,—a wondrous
world!

A wondrous world!
I can turn my eyes from it scarcely long enough to write
"Oh, Girl Scouts and their Leaders of Brooklyn,—a wondrous year
to you!"

Eleanor Roosevelt

1884–1962

Wife of Franklin Delano Roosevelt (32nd president), 1933–45

Eleanor Roosevelt was a courageous trailblazer. She was the first First Lady to hold regular news conferences, direct a government agency, attend a congressional hearing, testify before a congressional committee, and speak at a party's national convention. She was the first to travel on speaking tours and to represent the US overseas, visiting troops in England and the South Pacific during World War II. Her husband, Franklin Delano Roosevelt, died in office, and his successor, Harry S. Truman, named her the first American delegate to the United Nations. She championed that organization's Universal Declaration of Human Rights, and Truman praised her as the "First Lady of the World."

Eleanor was a prolific writer. While she was the First Lady, she began monthly and daily columns, which endured for nearly three decades. According to Allida M. Black in *Courage in a Dangerous World,* Eleanor penned "four autobiographies, seven monographs, seven children's books," and more than 100,000 letters.

When Eleanor was a child, her mother and aunts encouraged her affinity for poetry. She recalled that one aunt's reading of verse taught her that "poetry was sound and rhythm in addition to whatever meaning it might contain." As a student, she won awards for performing poetry that she memorized. In a school assignment, she said that a poet "must be conversant with all that is terribly awful and wonderfully beautiful," "able to admire alike what is splendidly great or elegantly small," and "acquainted with all the different modes of life." As an adult, she enjoyed reading poetry for hours at a time, and she recited poems dramatically.

Eleanor composed six poems while she was the First Lady. Two addressed her husband, and three were in correspondence to friends.

In addition to showing her personal side, the selections cover notable aspects of Roosevelt's presidency, including life at the White House and World War II.

Eleanor's 1937 memoir, *This Is My Story*, had been serialized. Before it was available as a book, she distributed bound sets of the previously published components. She inscribed her husband's copy with a comical quatrain, calling him "my dear."

At a birthday celebration for the president at the White House, Eleanor donned a chef's hat and recited a rhyming poem. She amusingly apologized for the unappetizing food. Overseeing the kitchen was the First Lady's least favorite responsibility, and plain fare was the norm.

In 1940, Eleanor published "Christmas—A Story," a fictional short story set during World War II. A six-line stanza interpolated into the story is from the perspective of a soldier "who thinks of" his wife and aims to "keep her safe." "Christmas—A Story" appears in *Eleanor Roosevelt's Christmas Book*, which was published posthumously and includes a chapter with her favorite verse about Christmas.

Two poems appeared in Eleanor's letters to Lorena Hickok. The friends exchanged more than 3,300 letters, beginning in 1932. The first poem was written in 1933, on the second day of Roosevelt's presidency. The second appeared on a "To My Valentine" card in 1935. Wording such as "my dear one" and "love" seems consistent with the inference from numerous biographers, historians, and journalists—based on many more revealing letters—that the two women had an affair.

"I urged that my mother's letters [to Hickok] be read in the context of those written to other close friends," retorted Franklin D. Roosevelt Jr. in the foreword of Joseph P. Lash's *Love, Eleanor*. Eleanor's son recruited her friend Lash to publish a collection of her letters. In the book, Lash recalled that, prior to Valentine's Day in 1941, Eleanor sent store-bought valentines. After Lash responded with his own poem, she offered two original stanzas. She appreciatively commended his verse and sent her love to his wife.

This may not look it but it is,
A book which will some day appear
It promises to be a whiz,
So little less you'll get my dear!

Duck, deer, salmon,
Turkey, pheasant, trout
Quail, moose and reindeer
All arriving by the ton
May be eaten with a pout
By the household, but the master
Never, never has enough.
On those who cook he's pretty rough
And when terrapin appears
Till he tastes it we're all ears
Fearing something wrong again,
But without these delicacies
Life would lose full half its flavor
So to the senders in these races
For the Presidential favor
Go his thanks and our apology
Mistress, housekeeper, and cook we're the sorry trilogy!

To a busy little housewife
From one who thinks of her through strife,
To keep her safe from all alarm
And never let her come to harm,
Is all he dreams of night and day
And now forever "Peace" would say.

Good night my dear one
Angels guard thee
God protect thee
My love enfold thee
All the night through.

May the world be full of sunshine,
And our meetings frequent be
Hours of joy & quiet time,
Take us over life's rough seas.

A lady read a valentine
Beneath a sky so blue
And spirits soared with every line
For words rang kind & true.

Your verse is far better than mine
But I ask that you take a bit of my heart
And share it with that Trude of thine,
And ever be grateful for Cupid's dart.

Michelle Obama

1964–

Wife of Barack Obama (44th president), 2009–17

Michelle Obama worked as an attorney in corporate law and public service roles. As First Lady, she dubbed herself "Mom in Chief," putting her parental responsibilities first. She advocated for military families and fought against childhood obesity. As part of her efforts to promote nutrition, she planted a vegetable garden on the grounds of the White House, which she covered in her debut book, *American Grown*.

After finishing her stint as First Lady, Michelle published two blockbuster nonfiction books, *Becoming* and *The Light We Carry*. Bolstered by a celebrity-moderated book tour that packed arenas, *Becoming* sold more than 18 million copies worldwide, making it the best-selling modern book by a former resident of the White House. Thanks to the audiobook versions of *Becoming* and *The Light We Carry*, Michelle is the only First Lady to win two Grammy Awards.

Around Valentine's Day in 2016, Michelle and her husband, Barack Obama, appeared on *The Ellen DeGeneres Show*. The president recited a comedic spoken word piece, in which he said, "I Obama*care* about you more than you even know!" The First Lady acknowledged that the coming Valentine's Day would be the last one in their current roles. She explained, "In honor of that, I wrote you a little Valentine's Day poem that I wanted to share." Her poem uses the "Roses are red" template, which dates back to 1784. This template can be found in myriad valentine cards and is frequently parodied in children's rhymes. The last line of the quatrain incorporates "boo," a slang term for "sweetheart."

Roses are red;
Violets are blue.
You are the president,
And I am your boo.

Appendix A: An Overview of Poetry by Jacqueline Kennedy Onassis

Jacqueline Kennedy Onassis's estate declined a request to include several of her previously published poems in this anthology. To read six of Jacqueline's poems, visit the bonus material webpage for *Poems by First Ladies* at www.doverpublications.com/0486853675. Links are provided for "Christmas," "Sea Joy," "Sailing," "Thoughts," "A Poem," and "Meanwhile in Massachusetts." "Sea Joy," "Thoughts," and "A Poem" are in Jacqueline's handwriting and feature her original illustrations.

Jacqueline's love for poetry began in her youth. Every Wednesday evening, she memorized poems with her grandfather. When she was eight, she composed her first poem, "Christmas," discussing Santa Claus, reindeer, snow, and merriness.

Growing up, she wrote poems for family members' anniversaries and her parents' birthdays. When her half sister was born, Jacqueline wrote a poem predicting that the baby would be the "First woman President."

In her early adolescence, Jacqueline wrote several poems that champion being on or by the water. In "Sea Joy," she professes that "to live by the sea is my only wish." In "Windy Song," she declares, "I could sail like this forever and ever." When Jacqueline was fourteen, her grandfather submitted "Sailing," a birthday poem she had written for him, to *The East Hampton Star*. "Sailing" concludes, "For the love of the sea is born in me/It will never let me go."

As a teenager, Jacqueline wrote two poems touting her preference for being alone. "Thoughts" addresses walking along the shore in the fall, "Where summer people were before/But now there's only me." "Song of the Night Watchman" celebrates being by herself to "walk the city in the rain." The latter is an example of the verse, short stories, and cartoons she contributed to *Salmagundy*, the school newspaper of which she was an editor.

In 1951, when Jacqueline was twenty-two, she and her sister, Lee, spent a summer traveling across Europe. Their account of the trip, including stories and drawings, was published as the book *One Special Summer* in 1974. Jacqueline penned the book's sole poem, which glorifies the sisters' gallivanting in Italy and France. The tongue-in-cheek "A Poem" takes up five pages and is accompanied by her drawings. Jacqueline says the sisters are "not at all what we seem to be." She contrasts propriety—going to church, writing to their mother, and supposedly turning in by 10 p.m.—with boisterous nightlife involving dancing, drinking, flirting, and kissing.

When Jacqueline was dating John Fitzgerald Kennedy, she wrote "Meanwhile in Massachusetts" about his presidential ambitions. It explains, "Part he must serve, a part he must lead/Both were his calling, both were his need." Kennedy's mother, Rose, felt that the "marvelous poem" won over some family members who had not yet made up their minds about Jacqueline.

Jacqueline passed along an affinity for poetry to her children. Her daughter Caroline Kennedy recalled that for holidays and birthdays, she and her brother had to compose or select a poem for their mother. They illustrated the poems and included them in a family scrapbook. Caroline later compiled *The Best-Loved Poems of Jacqueline Kennedy Onassis,* which features Jacqueline's favorite verse, discusses her feelings about poetry, and showcases three of her poems.

Jacqueline was proud of the Kennedy administration's promotion of poetry and the arts, Caroline noted in the book. "One of my mother's favorite White House events was an evening of Elizabethan poetry and music featuring the actor Basil Rathbone," Caroline said. "She worked hard on every detail of the evening . . . overruling the Library of Congress and other Shakespearean scholars to make sure that her favorite poems were included in the program."

Jacqueline's literary pursuits were wide-ranging. When she was in college, she "dreamed of writing the Great American Novel," as she put it. Around the time she graduated, her essays won *Vogue* magazine's

Prix de Paris contest. Prior to getting married, she was a newspaper reporter. She spent the last two decades of her life as a renowned book editor.

One of the last books Jacqueline worked on was *Skies in Blossom*, a handsome collection of Emily Dickinson's nature poetry. Mary Frank, who illustrated the book, recalled that Jacqueline "talked quite a bit about poetry, obviously not only knowledgeable, but, more interesting, with a real love and, I felt, a very real understanding."

Appendix B: "She Will Never Be a Poet": Polarizing Poetics About Hillary Clinton

Hillary Clinton has authored twelve books, more than any First Lady other than her heroine Eleanor Roosevelt. While Hillary's best-known works are adult nonfiction, she has written or cowritten a riveting novel, two picture books, a juvenile book about inspirational women, and a volume featuring children's letters to her dog and cat. I would not have been surprised to find an original poem in one of her books.

While she might not have written any verse, this creative writer does appreciate poetry. Hillary said she learned to "feel the music and rhythm and inspiration of poetry" by memorizing and reciting it in class in her youth. As a college senior, she quoted poems by T. S. Eliot and a friend in her thesis and graduation speech, respectively. As the First Lady, she praised "the timeless power of poetry and poets as our American memory, our purveyors of insight and culture, our eyes and ears who silence the white noise around us and express the very heart of what connects us, plagues us, and makes us fully human." She has interpolated poetry in her books and speeches.

To some, Hillary's essence is the epitome of poetry. To others, she is the antithesis.

Presidential Campaigns

This anthology focuses on verse, but *Merriam-Webster*'s alternate takes on "poetry" come into play. The second definition is "writing that formulates a concentrated imaginative awareness of experience in language chosen and arranged to create a specific emotional response through meaning, sound, and rhythm." The third is "something likened to poetry especially in beauty of expression."

During her primary battle against Senator Barack Obama in 2008, Hillary quoted Mario Cuomo, the former governor of New

York: "You campaign in poetry, but you govern in prose." She meant that, while Obama was an uplifting orator on the campaign trail, that did not necessarily translate to good governance. *The New Republic* said she might have written her campaign's "obituary" because she was "campaigning in prose" and had "left the poetry to" Obama. The Poetry Foundation said:

> When people criticize Clinton for failing to inspire, what they often mean is that she has no poetry about her. Her "story"—privileged upbringing, successful law career, singular focus on political ascendance—does not recommend itself to poetry. . . . Poets are allowed idealism and a degree of distance from mundane concerns. In her political career, Hillary Clinton has never allowed herself to be anything but defensive and practical. Obama, on the other hand, represents the middle ground between poet and politician; his idealism is essential to his political acumen.

The issue reappeared in the 2016 primary, contrasting Hillary's perceived staidness with Senator Bernie Sanders's flowery idealism. The month before the candidates' first debate, a *New York Times* op-ed called Hillary's campaign "the least romantic, poetic, and uplifting Democratic campaign in decades." *The Atlantic*'s David Frum rebutted, "Unpoetic? Hillary Clinton? No, no, no, and again no." Frum labeled Hillary's brand of poetry "darker, wilder, more dangerous, more interesting." After offering other thought-provoking examples, Frum concluded:

> It's . . . the poetry of the dutiful, the conscientious, the tidy, the punctual. They too have their hopes and aspirations—and also their disappointments, their resentments, their hatreds. Isn't it time somebody sung their story?

Shortly before the Iowa caucuses in 2016, Hillary said, "You know, look, you campaign in poetry, you govern in prose. And we need a lot more poetry in this campaign and in our country." The *Los Angeles Times* opined that Hillary "ignores the first half of Cuomo's advice: She campaigns almost entirely in prose. Her speeches are heavy with lists of medium-sized policy initiatives, but light on soaring dreams." Obama, the sitting president, chimed in that her "extraordinary" experience and intelligence "sometimes could make her more cautious and her campaign more prose than poetry, but those are also her strengths." *The New Yorker* asked, "But what might it mean if the language of campaigning—which is also the language of political participation—comes to seem almost entirely empty? Is that anyone's definition of poetry?"

Hillary's poetic nature or lack thereof even came up at the Democratic convention. Actor Ted Danson postulated, "Anybody can brag, anybody can talk. Hers is the poetry of doing." In response to her acceptance speech, *Vanity Fair* said, "She will never be a poet. But . . . Hillary Rodham Clinton nevertheless wrote the beginning of an eloquent new chapter in the nation's song of itself."

What the Poets Say

For someone whose biography supposedly "does not recommend itself to poetry," Hillary has inspired more poetry than might be expected. She is a muse for poets. Her story and her personality are grist for the mill. Some poetic treatments are laudatory, while others go in different directions.

The Hillary Clinton Quarterly published prose, poems, and cartoons about Hillary beginning in 1992. The poem "If Hillary Had Danced" imagines what her contributions would have been to the Age of Enlightenment and the French Revolution, saying that she would have fought for women's standing in society with "ballet grace." Other poems address topics ranging from the length of Hillary's hair to her role as a superheroine.

Hillary Clinton in Poems (2000) features selections from twenty-seven Nepali poets. The publisher's note explains that Hillary's "impressive personality" and her "responsibility" of advocating for women inspired the poems, which present "poetic beauty" about her "charismatic personality." Poems' titles include "Beautiful Hillary," "Hillary Clinton: A Perfect Woman," and "O Graceful Lady!" One selection imagines "If Hillary Rodhams multiply a little." One poem professes that she represents not just herself but "great America too," and one calls her "an exemplary institution" and "a source of poems." Another says that her "personality" led the poet to be "drenched in the shower of joy." Yet another praises, "America respects her, as someone with morals sound."

In *Hillary Clinton Haiku* (2015), Vera G. Shaw devotes a full book to haiku about Hillary. Shaw noted that the haiku "is the perfect vehicle to honor the simple elegance of the preeminent politician of our time." Shaw posited that "it is incontestable that Hillary Rodham Clinton's life is the stuff of poetry."

In *Hillary, Made Up* (2018), Marianne Kunkel serves up thirty-nine poems addressed to Hillary from the perspective of her beauty products. A blurb on the back cover explains that the cosmetic supplies suggest "ugly—and complicated—truths" about "gender and politics," regarding not just Hillary but "every woman who wants to be seen as more than just another pretty face." "Eyelash Curler to Hillary" expresses a desire for Hillary to "capture voters' hearts" as surely as an eyelash curler seizes eyelashes. "Retexturizing Cream to Hillary" explores how she glowed "with a youth that rivaled Obama's" at a primary debate in 2007. "Blow Dryer to Hillary" recalls when a hair dryer "drowned out your staff's gasps" when Sanders won the Michigan primary and "boomed over *boos*" when Donald Trump "mocked your pneumonia" in 2016. Dozens of personified eye, skin, and hair products show that poetic consideration of Hillary is deserved.

Found Poems

Some poets do more than write verse about Hillary. They adapt her words into poetry.

Found poems take someone else's words and convert them into poetry, such as by adding line breaks, stanza breaks, and indentations. In the following examples, Hillary's public statements in prose have been twisted into verse.

The Anthology of Really Important Modern Poetry (2012) is a treasure trove of found poems based on excerpts from politicians and other celebrities. The collection features two found poems lampooning Hillary. While the text of the found poem below uses Hillary's quotation verbatim, the title is contrived. Here is "A Poem of Denying Charges That I Asked My Former Aide to Fire White House Office Staff, or, Denial Is Not Just a River in Arkansas":

> He doesn't say I directly told him
>   anything.
> He says that,
> you know, the fact that I expressed
> concern
>   had an impact on him.
>   The mere expression of
>   concern
> could be, I guess, taken to
> mean something
> more
>   than it was meant.

Eight selections in *Hillary Clinton Haiku* are found poems. They are wholly enclosed in quotation marks and "are—more or less—true quotations," according to Shaw. For example, when Hillary conceded the 2008 primary, she said, "Although we weren't able to shatter that highest, hardest glass ceiling this time, thanks to you, it's got about 18 million cracks in it and the light is shining through like never before." Shaw's haiku version, titled "18 Million Cracks," is:

"Although we were not
able to shatter that glass,
light is shining through."

In 2015, Hillary's emails were a hot topic. *Newsweek*'s Zach Schonfeld "composed a found poem entirely from requests and questions emailed by Hillary Clinton (mostly to her staff)." Schonfeld called the poem a "tribute to the Dada nature of these brief dispatches." The poem retained Hillary's syntax and spelling but added capitalization and line breaks. The Dadaist poem combined quotations from distinct emails, devoid of context, in the same stanza and sometimes the same line. The quatrains mostly adhere to an *abab* rhyme scheme. The closing couplet reads, "'Pls print.' 'Pls print for me.' / 'Pls print for me and HAPPY EASTER!'"

As with her politics, views of Hillary's poetic alignment are polarized. It would have been unthinkable for most First Ladies to elicit such a voluminous and varied reaction, but it's no mystery why this one does. Following her time in the White House, Hillary was a senator, the secretary of state, and the first female presidential nominee of a major party, who won the popular vote. No other First Lady has a comparable résumé. Hillary's "life is the stuff of poetry," as Shaw put it, even if this isn't as "incontestable" as she claimed.

Appendix C: Close Calls for Eight Additional First Ladies

While I researched numerous other First Ladies, eight in particular caught my eye. Despite tantalizing breadcrumbs, I did not find poems by Abigail Adams, Priscilla Cooper Tyler, Abigail Fillmore, Ellen Wilson, Nancy Reagan, Barbara Bush, Laura Welch Bush, or Jill Biden.

Abigail Adams frequently quoted from poems in her letters. She lamented, "I wonder Apollo and the Muses could not have indulged me with a poetical Genious. I have always been a votary to her charms, but never could ascend Parnassus myself." I discovered a potentially original quatrain in a letter from Abigail to her sister Elizabeth. Gwen Fries, production editor for The Adams Papers, assessed that the lines were penned by a man Abigail mentioned in the letter. Fries confirmed that Abigail did not write any extant poetry.

When John Tyler's first wife, Letitia Tyler, was sick, she asked Priscilla Cooper Tyler, their daughter-in-law, to handle First Lady duties. Including when Letitia was ill and after she died, Priscilla served in this role for most of Tyler's presidency. According to *Priscilla Cooper Tyler and the American Scene, 1816–1889*, Priscilla "filled copy books with plays, poems, and stories of her own composition" in her youth. Considering that Priscilla also copied verse from known poets—including Lord Byron, Thomas Moore, and Percy Bysshe Shelley—in those books, I cannot conclude that any poems were original without seeing them. As of the 1950s, the only surviving volume, *Reflections of Celia*, was in the possession of Priscilla Goodwyn Griffin, the first Priscilla's granddaughter. I tracked down the second Priscilla's granddaughter, Priscilla Sands; the third Priscilla did not respond to my query. The Earl Gregg Swem Library at William & Mary Libraries, which houses the Tyler Family Papers, said that *Reflections of Celia* is not in their collection and did not know its whereabouts.

Abigail Fillmore, a teacher, was the first First Lady to work outside the home after getting married. The intellectual bibliophile established the White House's library. Holdings included volumes by Robert Burns and John Milton as well as *The Poets and Poetry of America* and *The Works of the British Poets Selected and Chronologically Arranged*. In one of the few extant letters from her ladyship, Abigail praised the book *Female Poets of America*, commending "the genius of my fellow country-women." She frequently quoted verse in her letters. Many of Abigail's papers were lost or destroyed. I expect that if this had not been the case, I would have found original poetry.

Ellen Wilson was an avid reader of poetry, delighting in the works of Elizabeth Barrett Browning, Robert Browning, and William Wordsworth. She often quoted from famous and lesser-known poets. Ellen and her husband, Woodrow Wilson, enjoyed reading poetry to each other. She was a painter and the author of several short stories, but despite due diligence, I could not verify that this poetry-loving artist tried her hand at verse.

A former Hollywood and Broadway actress, Nancy Reagan performed a skit at the Gridiron Dinner for journalists in 1982. The First Lady sang "Second-Hand Clothes," a rhyming parody of "Second-Hand Rose." Lyrics discussed a trench coat that "Ronnie"—Ronald Wilson Reagan—"bought for ten cents on the dollar" and asked, "Did Ronnie have to buy me that new sewing machine?" *The New York Times* raved that "no other First Lady had ever come [to the Gridiron Dinner] so well prepared with shtick, even including a mock piece of White House china for her to smash onstage." While the *Times* and other sources imprecisely called the lyrics "her own," the parody lyrics were written by Nancy's staff.

Barbara Bush's nickname was not meant to be taken seriously. In 1984, Barbara pejoratively described Geraldine Ferraro, George Bush's vice presidential opponent, as a "well, it rhymes with rich." In response, Barbara's family dubbed her the "Poet Laureate" of their household. As the First Lady, she launched the Barbara Bush Foundation for Family Literacy and championed the National Literacy Act.

Laura Welch Bush contributed to a poem in memory of a classmate in her high school yearbook, but she was apparently not the primary writer. As a teacher, she had her students write poems and create books of their own poetry. At the National Book Festival in 2003, the First Lady recited a poem that she said was written by her husband, George W. Bush. She later insisted that he had not written it. She might have, but this has never been confirmed. The Office of George W. Bush said, "Though Mrs. Bush does love reading poetry, we are unable to comment on whether or not she has authored any poems herself." The George W. Bush Presidential Library had me submit a Freedom of Information Act (FOIA) request that could take "months or years" to process; more than two years have passed.

Jill Biden has a master's in English and a doctorate in educational leadership. She taught college writing classes, and she had her students compose poems. Her poetry-loving husband, Joseph R. Biden, gifted her a book of original poems for Christmas in 2018 and adds a new poem by hand each year. At an event honoring student poets in 2022, the First Lady said, "In so many moments of my life, when my heart was bursting with an emotion that I couldn't quite describe—when I laid awake in the early morning hours, worry running through my mind—when I felt lost and utterly without a map, I turned to poetry." Both Katie Rogers, her biographer, and Vanessa Valdivia, her press secretary, were unaware of any poems Jill had written but agreed that my hunch was well-founded. Valdivia said she did not find any "public poetry," and her attempt to "see if there's anything else we can share" did not materialize. The Joseph R. Biden Jr. Presidential Library said that they could not "confirm whether there are poems written by Dr. Jill Biden within the Biden Presidential records" and I would not be able to submit a FOIA request for at least five years. Jill's onetime literary agent did not respond.

If I had my druthers, *Poems by First Ladies* would have included poetry from some of these First Ladies. Research obstacles got in the way.

Appendix D: Rose Elizabeth Cleveland's "George Eliot's Poetry"

Rose Elizabeth Cleveland's *George Eliot's Poetry and Other Studies* was published by Funk & Wagnalls in 1885, when she was the First Lady. Her fame helped this book of literary criticism and historical essays become a bestseller. Her debut had a dozen printings and earned her $25,000 in royalties. "No book of its kind has ever sold so well in this country," declared the publisher. One review called Rose "delightfully emphatic" and said the essays "glow with enthusiasm and will leave a vivid impression."

In the title essay, Rose pontificates about the verse of English writer George Eliot, who died in 1880. Rose passionately dismisses Eliot's poetic output as verse but not poetry. Rose opines, "Let verse have every quality which delights sense, captivates intellect, and stirs the heart, yet lack that ray which, coming from a sun beyond our system, reaches, blends with, vivifies, and assures the intimation of and longing for immortality in man—lacking this, you have not poetry."

The following is an abridged version of "George Eliot's Poetry."

George Eliot's Poetry

A genuine poem is almost certain of recognition, as such, in the long run. If verse contains poetry, that poetry makes itself felt, whatever blemishes the verse, as verse, may have; but if dint of argument alone brings us to acknowledge faultless verse a poem, like Galileo, in the moment of recantation, we shall mutter to ourselves our former and unrecanted conviction. Choose, for example, any Paris to arbitrate between "Aurora Leigh" and "The Spanish Gypsy," and which will win the golden apple? If Paris is at all able to tell black from white, he will at once perceive the "points" of which the "Gypsy" is possessed and of which "Aurora" is destitute. He will discover in the pages of George Eliot superlatives enough. Their color and glow, their vigor, their passion, their nobility of sentiment, their perfection of pathos, the sustained movement of the story, its tragic and worthy *dénouement*, its perfect prosody, its successful unities, and its atmosphere of ethical sublimity—all these will compare with "Aurora" to "Aurora's" disadvantage. And yet, "Aurora" gets the apple! Perhaps poor Paris can only stammer forth, in answer to the question, What in "Aurora" establishes her claim to the prize?—the unanswering answer, "*Je ne sais quoi.*" Paris knows that by the one he is impressed, stirred, uplifted; and that the other, with its high morality, rare knowledge, and brilliant diction, falls cold upon his ear; whether he comprehends it or not, it is the poetry in "Aurora" and the lack of it in the "Gypsy" which compels his decision.

I come at once to the consideration of George Eliot's verse in the mention of two qualities which it seems to me to lack, and which I hold to be essentials of poetry.

The first has to do with form, and is a property of the outside, that which affects and stops with the senses. Yet it is difficult to be exact. I ask myself, Is it her prosody? and am obliged to find it faultless as Pope's. There is never in her metres a syllable too much or too little.

Mrs. Browning's metre is often slovenly, her rhymes are often false. Yet Elizabeth Browning's verse has always poetry and music, which George Eliot's lacks.

What was work to write is work to read. Ruskin's dictum—"No great intellectual thing was ever done by great effort"—is pre-eminently true in the production of poetry. Poetry must be the natural manner of the poet, and can never be assumed. I do not mean to ignore the aids which study gives to genius; I only mean to say that no mere labor and culture can simulate poetic fire, or atone for its absence. George Eliot puts her wealth of message into the mould of poetic form by continuous effort.

George Eliot's prose carries easily its enormous burdens of concentrated gift. But poesy should betray no burdens. It should sport along its course and reach its goal unwearied.

The born poet has no agony in the deliverance of his song. The uttering is to him that soothing balm which the utterance is to his reader.

George Eliot has been said to possess Shakespearian qualities. Perhaps just here, in the relation of manner to matter, is seen her greatest resemblance and greatest difference. No writer ever carried and delivered so much as Shakespeare. Never was human utterance so packed with wealthy meaning, so loaded with all things that can be thought or felt, inferred or dreamed, as his. From one of his plays, replete with his incomparable wit, wisdom, and conceit, you emerge as from an ocean bath, exhilarated by the tossing of billows whose rough embrace dissolves to tenderest caress, yet carries in itself hints of central fire, of utmost horizon, of contact with things in heaven and earth undreamt of in our philosophy. You come from one of George Eliot's poems as from a Turkish bath of latest science and refinement,—appreciative of benefit, but so battered, beaten, and disjointed as to need repose before you can be conscious of refreshment.

A second quality which George Eliot's poetry lacks is internal, pertaining to matter rather than manner, though, standing, perhaps, in the relation to manner of cause to effect. It is that which all her works lack, but which prose can get along without; call it faith or transcendentalism; I prefer to define it negatively as the *antipode of agnosticism.*

Between all her lines is written the stern, self-imposed thus far and no farther. Her noblest characters move, majestic and sad, up to a—stone-wall!

Agnosticism can never exist in true poetry. Let verse have every quality which delights sense, captivates intellect, and stirs the heart, yet lack that ray which, coming from a sun beyond our system, reaches, blends with, vivifies, and assures the intimation of and longing for immortality in man—lacking this, you have not poetry.

It is the necessity of the poet, his *raison d'etre,* to meet and join the moving of men's minds toward the hereafter. We must not be confronted with silence; there must be recognition of this deepest yearning of the soul.

George Eliot answers sadly, with submission born of a proud ignorance, "I do not know. My feeling that there is something somewhere is, itself, unaccountable, and proves nothing. It is idle and impertinent to guess. There is that of which you and I both do know, because we have experience of it. Of this only will I speak. All else is but verbiage."

And she stops here, before a great stone-wall. There is no getting any farther. It is the very end.

Now, this can never be poetry; for the poet must ever open and widen our horizon.

Poetry can never leave the reader merely the stare of stone-dead, stone-blind eyes! It may give him absurd fancies, but it must give him something. It must not leave him to dwell with the silence of agnosticism.

George Eliot will not bid me hope when she has no assurance of the thing hoped for. "And here," she says, "is *the end!*" We may accept her dictum and be brave, silent, undeceived, and undeceiving agnostics; but we must say to her, "This is not poetry! It is the richest realism, presenting indubitable phenomena from which you draw, with strictest science, best deduction and inference concerning the known or the knowable. But, by virtue of all this, it is not poetry. The flattering lies and pretty guesses are not there, and will be missed. If you will persist in this sheer stop when you reach the confines of the known, you must not attempt to pass your work off as poetry. It is not so much that you do not know—nobody knows—as that you will not guess, or dream, or fancy, to their whim; that you will be so plainly, simply silent concerning the hereafter. Your readers will not endure that in poetry."

Perhaps these two qualities—the one extrinsic, as of the body; the other intrinsic, as of the mind; the one sensuous, the other spiritual—may not be distinguishable.

George Eliot's pages are a labyrinth of wonder and beauty; crowded with ethics lofty and pure as Plato's; with human natures fine and fresh as Shakespeare's; but a labyrinth in which you lose the guiding cord! With the attitude and utterance of her spirit confronting me, I cannot allow her verse to be poetry. She is the *raconteur*, not the *vates*; the scientist, not the seer.

Appendix E: Maury Madison, the Would-Be First Anthologizer

Composer Maury Madison compiled poems and "poetic prose" by presidents and First Ladies, primarily in the 1930s. In *Echoes of the White House,* Madison set the source material to music. *Bards of the White House* featured poems without musical arrangements. Neither collection was published in full, and a partial version of *Echoes of the White House* did not include any poems by First Ladies. Madison's manuscripts are held as part of the Maury Madison Papers at the Dolph Briscoe Center for American History at the University of Texas at Austin.

Madison included verse from six First Ladies: Dolley Madison, Louisa Adams, Julia Tyler, Mary Todd Lincoln, Grace Coolidge, and Lou Hoover. In 1931, the Associated Press reported that the composer sought "to unearth enough lyrics written by White House mistresses to make a booklet of song." He assessed that Lou Hoover's "Recollections of a Piece of Wood" would be difficult to set to music but would be "a lovely little song."

He published individual scores for three poems by Grace Coolidge: "The Open Door," "The Quest," and "Watch-Fires." The score for "The Quest" is provided beginning on the next page.

The Quest

Medium Key

Written on the lines of the poem by
GRACE COOLIDGE
(Mrs. Calvin Coolidge)

Music by
MAURY MADISON

cresc.
night
Scal - ing the
p
cresc.
face of the peak of dreams, We
en - ter the reg - ions of light,
L.H.
mf
And hast - 'ning on, with

cresc.
eag - er in - tent Ar - rive at the
rain - bow's end And there un -
cov - er the pot of gold Bur - ied deep in the
heart of a friend.
mf
f
rall.
pp
8va

Appendix F: Poems About First Ladies by Presidents

While this anthology highlights poems by First Ladies, it is notable that six presidents devoted poetic treatment to a common subject: First Ladies. The two focuses dovetail nicely.

Selections from John Quincy Adams, John Tyler, and Woodrow Wilson appear below. Poems by Jimmy Carter, William J. Clinton, and Joseph R. Biden are discussed, with excerpts, but the full text is not included due to practical obstacles. For more information about presidents' relationships with poetry, see *Poems by Presidents: The First-Ever Anthology*.

John Quincy Adams

John Quincy Adams, the most prolific poet among presidents, wrote about 350 surviving poems. He published an epic poem, *Dermot Mac Morrogh, or The Conquest of Ireland*, and a collection of his verse, *Poems of Religion and Society*, was published shortly after his death. While many of his poems were religious, he wrote about such far-ranging subjects as his father's legacy, a comet, and a balloon flight. In "To My Wife," he affectionately addresses his wife, Louisa, the most prolific poet among First Ladies. He declares that while ten thousand other women "might as sweetly smile," "their smiles beam not on" him. He likely wrote the poem in 1816, when they had been married for nearly two decades.

To My Wife

Friend of my bosom! dearest wife!
With rapture I receive thy lays.
From thee, best solace of my life,
How charming is the voice of praise!
What though the Conscience in my breast
Thy bright but partial tints disclaim:
It knows, thy Bosom was the test,
Whence the too vivid colours came.

Alas! dear Wife, full well I know
That in my person and mind
Ten blemishes would strike a foe
For each perfection thou canst find.
Should'st thou to vanity give birth,
Her whispers shall reflection lend,
'Tis not the Portrait of my worth,
'Tis but the Pencil of a Friend.

Nigh twenty years of lengthen'd span.
On Earth their destin'd course have run,
Since, in the face of God and man,
Thy lot and mine, were link'd in one.
Louisa! could a mortal hand,
Break for a moment, Thy men's chain,
Before the Altar I would stand.
And thou shouldst be, my Bride again.

Not that thy face albeit fair
  Displays perfection never seen:
Not that thy form could ever dare
  To rival Beauty's matchless Queen.
Ten thousand Maids o'er Britain's Isle
  In Beauty might have vied with thee.
Ten thousand might as sweetly smile;
  But ah! their smiles beam not on me!

Thy heart is generous and kind—
  Of Woman 'tis the common pride:
Pure as the vital air thy mind,
  As pure ten thousand minds beside.
Base were the tribute that should prize
  Worth as if lent to me alone;
And all thy sex's charms despise
  By falsehood to extol thy own.

Ah! not on falsehood's fleeting sand
  The virtues rest that grac'd thy youth.
Firm on a lasting base they stand;
  The Adamantine Rock of Truth
And what are to thy Lover's eye,
  The Beauties other damsels boast?
Trust me they pass unheeded by,
  Or raise a transient glance at most.

But thine are grappled to my soul;
  They beat in every throbbing vein;
Warm with the tide of life they roll;
  They tune my nerves, inspire my brain:
Nor, to this perishable day,
  Can their impression rest confin'd.
Thought, Memory, Fancy feel their sway;
  They fill the never dying mind.

Yes, Dearest, when my latest Breath
  'Tis dust to dust shall soon restore,
Thy image living yet in death,
  With me to yonder skies shall soar.
And when the trumpets sound at last,
  The universal dead shall rear,
My Soul, responsive to the blast,
  With thine Louisa, shall appear.

Then as we tremble and rejoice,
  Be thy last doom and mine the same.
And, may the dread Archangel's voice,
  Our final sentence thus proclaim.
"Refin'd from dross go, spirits go,
  "Forever blest in mutual Love!
"And let your purest joy, below,
  "Be still your endless joys above."

John Tyler

John Tyler was president for less than one full term. During his presidency, his first wife, Letitia, died, and he courted his second wife, Julia, who was three decades his junior. Prior to becoming the first president to get married while in office in 1844, Tyler wrote two poems for Julia. In *And Tyler Too,* Robert Seager II explained that Tyler was smitten with Julia's "beauty, vivacity, good humor, and poise" and that when he "was happy, poetry invariably flowed from his lips and from his pen." He penned "Sweet Lady, Awake!" in 1843 and revised it during their honeymoon, and Julia set it to music. Seager deemed it "the only known musical collaboration" between a president and a First Lady. After Tyler wrote "Shall I again that Harp unstring" in her autograph album, Supreme Court Justice Henry Baldwin saw the poem and shared it, prompting gossip about Tyler's intention to remarry in political circles.

Sweet Lady, Awake!
A Serenade Dedicated to Miss Julia Gardiner

Sweet lady awake, from your slumbers awake,
Weird beings we come o'er hill and through brake
To sing you a song in the stillness of night,
Oh, read you our riddle fair lady aright?
We are sent by the one whose fond heart is your own,
Who mourns in thy absence and sighs all alone.
Alas, he is distant—but tho' far, far away,
He thinks of you, lady, by night and by day.
Sweet lady awake, sweet lady awake!

His hearth, altho' lonely, is bright with your fame,
And therefore we breathe not the breath of his name.
For oh! if your dreams have response in your tone,
Long since have you known it as well as your own.
We are things of the sea, of the earth, and the air,
But ere you again to your pillow repair,
Entrust us to say you gave ear to our strain,
And were *he* the minstrel you would listen again.
Sweet lady awake, sweet lady awake!

Woodrow Wilson

In 1884, for her twenty-fifth birthday, Woodrow Wilson praised his "lady fair," Ellen Louise Axson, in "To E. L. A. on Her Birthday." In *Woodrow Wilson: The Last Romantic*, Mary Stockwell wrote that Wilson "could not find the words that captured how wonderful he thought she truly was," as some of his wording "seemed to pale in comparison to the reality of the young woman he loved so much." The couple wed the following year.

To E. L. A. on Her Birthday

I cannot tell, my lady fair,
What thine own thoughts may be
When that thou comest once again
Thy natal day to see;

But this I know, and fain would tell
Close at thy listening ear,
That God has given few gifts more blest
Than this thy closing year.

Bright as thy frank and laughing eyes
Should be this blest May-day,
And radiant as thy loving smile
Its sun's flower-kissing ray.

Thy sorrows past are hallowed all
By deeds of duteous love;
They speak to thee of gladness given
To that dear one above.

They testify of love's glad care
For duties thou did'st bear
To make thy home again as bright
As when her form was there.

That home was stricken, not in wrath
For sin, or shame, or wrong,
But that in God our trust might stand
And in his strength be strong.

Why should'st thou not thy birthday hail
With joy and hope and mirth?
How sad soe'er thy life has been
God smiled upon thy birth.

For thee he sent to blessings bear
Of love and sympathy,
To show to us the beauty rare
Of brave work's majesty.

He sent thee to make bright the lives
And ease the arduous part
Of those to whom thou wast to bring
Thy purity of heart.

He gave to thee in largess free
Not only beauty's charm,
But all the graces that win man
And stay him from his harm.

Thou art thyself his chiefest gift
To him to whom 'tis given
To see in thy sweet, trusting eyes
The love for which he's striven.

If that thou think'st it good to be
On such blest missions sent,
Can'st thou not smile e'en o'er the year
That's been so sadly spent?

This fair May-day sure seems to me
A rose without its thorn;
For can there be aught ill in this,
The day when thou wast born?

Until I saw thy winsome face
And love-light in thine eyes,
I had not known the fairest forms
Born 'neath these May-day skies.

But now I can believe that this,
The hey-day of the Spring,
Is fairest month in Nature's round
For that it thee did bring!

Jimmy Carter

When Jimmy Carter was in the Navy in 1948–52, he spent long stretches on a submarine and wrote verse to help pass the time, including love poems for his wife, Rosalynn. In 1995, Carter published the *New York Times* bestseller *Always a Reckoning and Other Poems*, the only collection of poems by a president published in his lifetime. The book was dedicated, in part, "to Rosalynn, who, most of all, has stretched my mind and heart and let me know what patience, love, and sharing mean." In "Rosalynn," he celebrates that even in old age, Rosalynn's "smile still makes the birds forget to sing/and me to hear their song." In "Some Things I Love," he vows to love her until "what rhymes with breath."

William J. Clinton

The 2018 thriller *The President Is Missing*, cowritten by William J. Clinton and James Patterson, includes a three-stanza poem. As part of a flashback, a future president, Jonathan Duncan, recites a rhyming poem to his future wife, Rachel Carson. The protagonist says that while he should be studying "equal protection, the law and racial quotas," he is fixated on "a green-eyed girl from Minnesota." Carson acknowledges that the Minnesota rhyme is "impressive."

The scene is inspired by how the Clintons met in the library of Yale Law School, where he stared at her and she introduced herself.

In the novel, the starting point for the couple's courtship occurs at their law school's library, where Duncan shares his verse.

Although the poem is about a fictional First Lady, Carson is reminiscent of Hillary Clinton. Hillary and Carson grew up in the Midwest, and both attended college in Massachusetts. As with the Clintons, Carson is ahead of Duncan in law school. Hillary was on the board of editors for Yale's law review, and Carson is the editor in chief of the law review. The moniker Rachel Carson is a nod to a biologist of the same name; her book *Silent Spring*, which Hillary has praised, spurred the environmental movement.

Although Clinton is credited as the primary author of *The President Is Missing*, it is unclear to what extent he composed the poem or provided guidance for it. The only part of the book that Clinton wrote single-handedly was a speech toward the end.

Joseph R. Biden

In 2018, Joseph R. Biden gave his wife, Jill, a book of original poems as a Christmas gift. Her favorite includes this couplet: "I worked so hard to get you to say I do/When you did—you made the world anew." During a television interview in 2022, she revealed that he adds a new poem to the book by hand for Christmas annually. "I have a lot to write about," said the president as he grabbed her hand.

Selected Bibliography

This bibliography is not a complete record of all works and sources. Readers who are interested in the most significant literature about poems by First Ladies and related topics should read the following.

Anthony, Carl Sferrazza. *As We Remember Her: Jacqueline Kennedy Onassis in the Words of Her Family and Friends*. HarperCollins, 1997.

Anthony, Carl Sferrazza. *Camera Girl: The Coming of Age of Jacqueline Bouvier Kennedy*. Gallery Books, 2023.

Anthony, Carl Sferrazza. *First Ladies: The Saga of the Presidents' Wives and Their Power, 1789–1961*. William Morrow and Company, Inc., 1990.

Anthony, Carl Sferrazza. *First Ladies: The Saga of the Presidents' Wives and Their Power, 1961–1990*. Vol. II. William Morrow and Company, Inc., 1991.

Anthony, Carl Sferrazza. "First Lady as Author." National First Ladies Library. Accessed May 22, 2023. http://archive.firstladies.org/blog/first-ladies-as-author/.

Anthony, Carl Sferrazza. *Florence Harding: The First Lady, the Jazz Age, and the Death of America's Most Scandalous President*. William Morrow and Company, Inc., 1998.

Anthony, Carl Sferrazza. *Nellie Taft: The Unconventional First Lady of the Ragtime Era*. William Morrow, 2005.

Bouvier, Jacqueline, and Lee Bouvier. *One Special Summer*. Rizzoli, 2006.

Brower, Kate Andersen. *First Women: The Grace and Power of America's Modern First Ladies*. Harper, 2016.

Carlin, Diana B., Anita B. McBride, and Nancy Kegan Smith. *U.S. First Ladies: Making History and Leaving Legacies*. Cognella, 2024.

Cleveland, Rose Elizabeth. *George Eliot's Poetry and Other Studies*. Funk & Wagnalls, 1885.

Croland, Michael, ed. *Poems by Presidents: The First-Ever Anthology*. Dover Publications, 2023.

Ehrenhalt, Lizzie, and Tilly Laskey, eds. *Precious and Adored: The Love Letters of Rose Cleveland and Evangeline Simpson Whipple, 1890–1918*. Minnesota Historical Society Press, 2019.

Emerson, Jason, ed. *Lincoln's Lover: Mary Lincoln in Poetry*. The Kent State University Press, 2018.

Gould, Lewis L., ed. *American First Ladies: Their Lives and Their Legacy*. 2nd ed. Routledge, 2001.

Graham, Judith S., Beth Luey, Margaret A. Hogan, and C. James Taylor. *Diary and Autobiographical Writings of Louisa Catherine Adams*. The Belknap Press of Harvard University Press, 2013.

Hogan, Margaret A., and C. James Taylor. *A Traveled First Lady: Writings of Louisa Catherine Adams*. The Belknap Press of Harvard University Press, 2014.

Kennedy, Caroline, ed. *The Best-Loved Poems of Jacqueline Kennedy Onassis*. Hyperion, 2001.

Kuhn, William. *Reading Jackie: Her Autobiography in Books*. Nan A. Talese/Doubleday, 2010.

Kunkel, Marianne. *Hillary, Made Up*. Stephen F. Austin University Press, 2018.

Lash, Joseph P. *Love, Eleanor: Eleanor Roosevelt and Her Friends*. Doubleday, 1982.

Lawrence, Greg. *Jackie as Editor: The Literary Life of Jacqueline Kennedy Onassis*. Thomas Dunne Books, 2011.

Morris, Sylvia Jukes. *Edith Kermit Roosevelt: Portrait of a First Lady*. The Modern Library, 1980.

Pudasaini, Kanchan, ed. *Hillary Clinton in Poems*. Vishnu-Chandra Vangmaya Mandir, 2000.

Real Calvin Coolidge. No. 10. The Calvin Coolidge Memorial Foundation, Inc., 1994.

Rogers, Katie. *American Woman: The Transformation of the Modern First Lady, from Hillary Clinton to Jill Biden.* Crown, 2024.

Roosevelt, Eleanor. *Eleanor Roosevelt's Christmas Book.* Dodd, Mead & Company, 1963.

Salenius, Sirpa. *Rose Elizabeth Cleveland: First Lady and Literary Scholar.* Palgrave Macmillan, 2014.

Schneider, Dorothy, and Carl J. Schneider. *First Ladies: A Biographical Dictionary.* 3rd ed. Facts on File, 2010.

Seager, Robert, II. *And Tyler Too: A Biography of John & Julia Gardiner Tyler.* McGraw-Hill Book Company, Inc., 1963.

Shaw, Vera G. *Hillary Clinton Haiku: Her Rise to Power, Syllable by Syllable, Pantsuit by Pantsuit.* Twelve, 2015.

Singer, Marilyn. *Have You Heard About Lady Bird? Poems About Our First Ladies.* Disney Hyperion, 2018.

Streitmatter, Rodger, ed. *Empty Without You: The Intimate Letters of Eleanor Roosevelt and Lorena Hickok.* The Free Press, 1998.

Thomas, Louisa. *Louisa: The Extraordinary Life of Mrs. Adams.* Penguin Press, 2016.